BLUE BONNET'S RANCH PARTY

A SEQUEL TO A TEXAS BLUE BONNET

C. E. JACOBS

AND EDYTH ELLERBECK READ

1ˢᵗ WORLD
LIBRARY
Literary Society

Blue Bonnet's Ranch Party

C. E. Jacobs & Edyth Ellerbeck Read

© 1st World Library, 2007
PO Box 2211
Fairfield, IA 52556
www.1stworldlibrary.com
First Edition

LCCN: 2007934090

Softcover ISBN: 978-1-4218-9628-1
Hardcover ISBN: 978-1-4218-9728-8
eBook ISBN: 978-1-4218-9528-4

Purchase *"Blue Bonnet's Ranch Party"*
as a traditional bound book at:
www.1stWorldLibrary.com/purchase.asp?ISBN=978-1-4218-9628-1

1st World Library is a literary, educational organization
dedicated to:

- Creating a free internet library of downloadable ebooks

- Hosting writing competitions and offering book publishing
scholarships.

Interested in more 1st World Library books? contact:
literacy@1stworldlibrary.com
Check us out at: www.1stworldlibrary.com

1st World Library Literary Society

Giving Back to the World

"If you want to work on the core problem, it's early school literacy."

- James Barksdale, former CEO of Netscape

"No skill is more crucial to the future of a child, or to a democratic and prosperous society, than literacy."

- Los Angeles Times

"Literacy... means far more than learning how to read and write... The aim is to transmit... knowledge and promote social participation."

- UNESCO

"Literacy is not a luxury, it is a right and a responsibility. If our world is to meet the challenges of the twenty-first century we must harness the energy and creativity of all our citizens."

- President Bill Clinton

"Parents should be encouraged to read to their children, and teachers should be equipped with all available techniques for teaching literacy, so the varying needs and capacities of individual kids can be taken into account."

- Hugh Mackay

CONTENTS

CHAPTER I

THE WANDERER

BLUE BONNET put her head out of the car window for the hundredth time that hour, and drew it back with a sigh of utter exasperation.

"Uncle Cliff," she declared impatiently, "if The Wanderer doesn't move a little faster I'll simply have to get out and push!"

"Better blame the engine, Honey," said Uncle Cliff in his slow, soothing way. "The Wanderer is doing her best. Might as well blame the wagon for not making the horses gallop!"

"I know," she confessed. "But it seems as if we'd never get to Woodford. This is the longest-seeming journey I ever took— even if it is in a private car." Then, fearing to appear inappreciative, she added quickly: "But I do think it is mighty good of Mr. Maldon to let us take his very own car. I can just see the We are Sevens' eyes pop right out when they see this style of travelling." Blue Bonnet's own eyes roamed over the luxurious interior of The Wanderer, dwelling with approval on the big, swinging easy chairs, the book-case cunningly set in just over a writing-desk, the buffet shining with cut glass and silver, and the thousand and one details that made the car a veritable palace on wheels.

Blue Bonnet had been spending a few days in New York with her uncle, who had insisted that she should have a little "lark" after her long months in school. Now, in a private car belonging to one of Uncle Cliff's friends, they were on their way back to Woodford, there to gather up Grandmother Clyde, Alec Trent, and the other six of Blue Bonnet's "We are Seven" Club, and bear them off to Texas for the summer.

"I reckon Sarah Blake and Kitty Clark aren't very used to travelling?" suggested Uncle Cliff, more to draw out Blue Bonnet than with any consuming desire for information.

"Used to travelling! Why, Uncle Cliff—" Blue Bonnet shook her head emphatically—"not one of the other We are Sevens has ever so much as seen the inside of a Pullman in all her life!"

Mr. Ashe hid a smile under his moustache. The fact that Blue Bonnet's own introduction to a Pullman car had occurred just nine months before, seemed to have escaped the young lady's mind.

"Well, well," ejaculated Blue Bonnet's uncle, "they've some experiences ahead of them, to be sure!"

"Oh, Uncle,"—Blue Bonnet was struck with a sudden fear,— "do you suppose they will all be ready to go? We're two whole days earlier than we said we'd be—"

"They'll be ready, don't you worry. Your grandmother is not one of the unprepared sort, and the girls don't need much of a wardrobe for the ranch. Besides, I wired them explicit directions—to meet The Wanderer and be ready to come aboard immediately. We shall have only a few minutes in Woodford."

C. E. Jacobs & Edyth Ellerbeck Read

Blue Bonnet settled back in her red velvet reclining chair and shut her eyes. Slowly a smile wreathed her lips.

"What's the joke, Honey?"

Blue Bonnet looked up with dancing eyes. "Benita!" she laughed. "Won't she be just—petrified, when she sees seven girls instead of one? And can't you imagine the boys—"

"Benita had better not get petrified this summer," interrupted Uncle Cliff. "She has to do some tall hustling. I've wired Uncle Joe to get extra help while the ranch party is in session. If they can get old Gertrudis from the Lone Star Ranch—she's the finest cook in the state of Texas. And her granddaughter might wait on table."

"Oh, I do think a ranch party is the grandest thing in the world," cried Blue Bonnet. "I've read of house parties, but they must be downright tame compared with this kind of a party. And it's not to last just over a week-end either, but *two whole months*! Why, Uncle Cliff, any ordinary man would be scared to pieces at the prospect."

"But I'm not an ordinary man, eh?" Mr. Ashe looked pleased as a boy as he put the question.

"Well, I reckon not! You're a fairy godfather. You grant my wishes before they're fairly out of my mouth. And I seem to have plenty of wishes. Just think, Uncle, how many things I've wished for since my last birthday!"

"First," said Uncle Cliff, "you wished to go away from the ranch."

Blue Bonnet nodded assent. "Because I was—afraid—to ride. Doesn't it seem ridiculous, now I'm over that silliness?

But oh, how I did wish I could get over being afraid! That was about the only wish you couldn't grant, Uncle Cliff."

"That wish was never expressed, Honey—don't forget that. Maybe I could have helped even there," Mr. Ashe suggested gently.

"I know, it was my own fault. But I was—ashamed, Uncle Cliff. You don't suppose—" Blue Bonnet's face clouded, "you don't think, do you, that the fear will come again when I get back where I saw Jose—dragged?" She shut her eyes and shuddered.

"Nonsense, Honey. That fear died and was buried the day you rode Alec's horse, Victor. A good canter on Firefly over the Blue Bonnet country will make you wonder that such a feeling was ever born."

"Dear old Firefly! Won't I make it up to him though! Isn't it queer how many of my wishes have come true? It makes me feel almost—breathless. I no sooner got through wishing I could leave the ranch and go East and be with Grand-mother—than I woke up in Woodford. And I wanted—thought I wanted—to be called Elizabeth. Blue Bonnet became Elizabeth!"

"A real lightning change artist," murmured Uncle Cliff.

"And I wanted to go to school. Granted. I wanted to know a lot of girls, and behold the We are Sevens!"

"And when was it you changed names again?" Uncle Cliff asked slyly.

"When I got tired of being Elizabethed. Everybody thinks Blue Bonnet suits me better, except Aunt Lucinda—

C. E. Jacobs & Edyth Ellerbeck Read

on occasions."

"And the next wish? They're stacking up."

"I reckon it was about the Sargent prize in school. I wanted Alec Trent to win it—and he did. And next I wished to pass my school examinations—"

"And even that miracle was achieved!" said Uncle Cliff, pinching her cheek.

"And, finally, I wanted to go back to Texas, and, at the same time, I wished I didn't have to leave Grandmother and Alec and the girls. That might seem a contrary pair of wishes, but it doesn't daunt Godfather Ashe. He straightway makes a private car arise from—from what, Uncle Cliff?"

"Tobacco smoke," promptly supplied Mr. Ashe, with a reminiscent smile on his lips.

"Why tobacco smoke?" asked Blue Bonnet wonderingly.

"I taught Maldon to smoke when he was a young chap visiting out our way, and we've been friends ever since. The private car seems to have grown out of that," replied her uncle.

"I see," Blue Bonnet nodded. "But don't tell Aunt Lucinda,— I fancy she doesn't approve of smoking."

"So I've noticed," rather grimly rejoined Mr. Ashe. Blue Bonnet's prim New England aunt had not suffered him to remain long in ignorance of her disapproval of tobacco in any form.

"There's one thing I don't understand at all," Blue Bonnet

knitted her pretty brows. "And that is what was in Uncle Joe Terry's telegram the other day. Won't you tell me, Uncle?"

"Nothing much,—only that I must be back at the ranch Monday evening without fail," answered Uncle Cliff with an air of evasion.

"There's some deep reason, I can just feel it. You mean well, Uncle, but I just hate secrets." Blue Bonnet laid a coaxing hand on her uncle's arm.

"Secret indeed!" scoffed Uncle Cliff, avoiding his niece's eye.

"You can't pretend a bit well," Blue Bonnet assured him gravely. "You look just the way my dog Solomon does when he's pretending to be asleep—and can't keep his tail from wagging!"

"Thank you!" said Uncle Cliff with well-assumed indignation.

"You're quite welcome. He's a mighty wise dog, Uncle Cliff—that's why I named him Solomon. You know I think—" Blue Bonnet went on sagely, "I think there is some trouble at the ranch,—because I saw the big box you sent with our trunks and it was labelled 'dangerous.' Now, be nice, and tell me what was in it."

"I understood that Miss Kitty was the inquisitive member of your Club," Uncle Cliff parried provokingly.

Blue Bonnet sighed. "Well, I can thank Uncle Joe for cutting us out of two whole days in New York. I'm sure Aunt Lucinda will be disappointed."

"Aunt Lucinda—?" echoed Mr. Ashe.

"Yes, you see it was this way: Aunt Lucinda gave me a list of things I ought to see in New York. Every day when you asked me 'what next?'—as you did, you nice fairy godfather—I chose the things I'd rather see and left the—the educational things for the last. You see the shops, the Hippodrome, Coney Island, Peter Pan and the Goddess of Liberty were so fascinating, and I'd wanted so long to see them, that—Well, to face the bitter truth, Uncle Cliff, we left New York without one weenty peek in at the Metropolitan Museum!"

"Horrors!" Uncle Cliff looked properly stunned. Then he said craftily, "Keep it dark, Honey. Maybe we can bluff."

Blue Bonnet shook her head. "Nobody can bluff Aunt Lucinda—I ought to know! Why—Uncle Cliff—I believe we're there!"

And "there" they certainly were. While Blue Bonnet had been busily chattering, The Wanderer had drawn in to the Woodford station.

Half the population of the village was assembled on the platform, it seemed to Blue Bonnet as she sprang from the car steps. Grandmother and Aunt Lucinda she saw first, and back of them Denham, the coachman, bearing suitcases, umbrellas, magazines and wraps, besides holding on by main force to a leash at which Solomon was straining frantically. Beside him were Katie and Delia, on hand for a final farewell to Blue Bonnet and Mrs. Clyde. Then came Kitty and Doctor Clark; Amanda and the Parkers; Sarah and the whole crowd of Blakes, big and little; Alec and the General; Debby, and a collection of sisters, cousins, uncles and aunts that overflowed the platform and straggled clear out to the line of hitching-posts, where all of Woodford's family conveyances seemed drawn up at once.

The report of Blue Bonnet's ranch party had spread like wildfire through the town, and the going away of so many of its most prominent citizens to far-off Texas, had aroused quiet Woodford to a pitch of excitement equalled only by that of a prohibition election, or a visit from the President.

Blue Bonnet was swallowed up by the crowd the moment she alighted, and it was a full five minutes before she emerged, flushed and minus her hat, to ask breathlessly, "Oh, is everybody here?—I can't see anybody for the crowd!"

"No time to lose," warned Mr. Ashe. "We must pull out in ten minutes in order to reach Boston in time for the 5.17 to-night."

Even as he spoke, The Wanderer began to move.

"Uncle Cliff," cried Blue Bonnet in a panic, "they're going without us!"

"Just switching," soothed her uncle. "The Wanderer has to be on the other track so as to hook on to the train for Boston. That's due in five minutes. Get your good-byes said so that everybody can go aboard when she comes alongside."

During that five minutes while each girl was occupied with her own family, Blue Bonnet had a moment alone with her aunt. "It's a good thing we said our real good-bye before I went to New York, isn't it, Aunt Lucinda?" she asked, slipping her hand shyly into that of her tall, prim aunt. Somehow Aunt Lucinda had never seemed so dear as in this moment of parting. Perhaps it was the look as of unshed tears in her eyes, or the flush on her usually pale face that made her seem more approachable. Blue Bonnet could not

C. E. Jacobs & Edyth Ellerbeck Read

tell exactly what it was, but there was a vague something about Aunt Lucinda that made her appear almost—yes, almost, pathetic. Suddenly Blue Bonnet remembered—they were leaving Aunt Lucinda all alone. Her heart reproached her. "Aunt Lucinda," she whispered hurriedly, "won't you come, too?"

One of her rare sweet smiles lit Miss Clyde's face. "Thank you, dear—it is sweet of you to want me. But not this time, for I have promised friends to go abroad with them. I shall miss you, Blue Bonnet,—you won't forget to write often?"

"No, indeed!" Blue Bonnet assured her, at the same moment registering a solemn vow that she would write every week without fail. "And you'll write too, Aunt Lucinda? It'll be so exciting getting letters from funny, foreign places. And now it's good-bye. You—you are sure you've no—a—advice to give me?"

Miss Clyde restrained an odd smile at the significant question. "No, dear. Only this: be considerate of your grand-mother, and bring her back safely to me."

"I will! I will!" cried Blue Bonnet, and with another kiss was gone.

There was only a moment for a handshake with Katie and Delia, who openly mopped their eyes at parting; a word with General Trent, a chorus of good-byes to a score of We are Seven relations, and then everybody crowded about the steps of The Wanderer.

"Grandmother first," said Blue Bonnet. "Denham, you'd better go aboard and get her settled. Here, Bennie Blake— you hold Solomon till I'm ready to take him. Now then, We are Sevens—forward!"

Suddenly Blue Bonnet gave a queer little exclamation and clapped her hand on a leather case which hung from her shoulder. "Stop, everybody, till I get a picture—I nearly forgot! And I want pictures of every stage of the ranch party. Grandmother, please stay on the top step and I'll group the girls below."

"That's right," cried Kitty. "Take one now and another when we get back, and we can label them 'Before and After Taking!'"

Sarah, Kitty, Amanda and Debby, amid the teasing remarks of sundry small boys, obediently took their places as designated by the young artist. Then Blue Bonnet's eyes turned in search of the other two girls.

"Susy! Ruth!" she called. "Why—where are they?"

An embarrassed hush fell on the group about the car. Blue Bonnet looked inquiringly at the telltale faces. It did not take her long to scent a mystery.

"What's the matter?" she cried impatiently.

Doctor Clark stepped forward, clearing his throat queerly. "Fact is, Miss Blue Bonnet," he began, "they—they can't go."

"Can't go?" Blue Bonnet started incredulously at the stammering doctor.

"No, you see,—well, in fact, they're ill," he completed lamely. Why didn't some one help him out, the doctor fumed inwardly, instead of letting him be the one to cloud that beaming face?

16   C. E. Jacobs & Edyth Ellerbeck Read

Suddenly Kitty leaned down from the car step and whispered: "Scarlet fever!"

"Both?" exclaimed the startled Blue Bonnet.

"No, only Ruth. But Susy was exposed and Father didn't think it safe for her to come."

"Oh, Kitty!" The tears sprang to Blue Bonnet's eyes—she fought them but they would come.

"We're all broken up over it," said Kitty with her own lips trembling; "but it might have been worse. It's only because we've been too busy to go out there, that we weren't all exposed. Then it would have been good-bye to the ranch party."

"Oh, Kitty, suppose you had!" The thought of the narrow escape dried Blue Bonnet's tears. "I'm mighty glad you four could come. But it won't be complete. And you know how I love to have things complete!"

"Never mind, Blue Bonnet, you still have me!" cried Alec, coming in with a cheerful note.

"'The poor ye have always with you!'" chimed in Kitty, and while everybody was laughing over this sally, Blue Bonnet took a snap-shot of the group, and then all the travellers trooped aboard.

Mr. Ashe looked over the heads of the chattering crowd in the car and met Mrs. Clyde's amused eye. "How do you like mothering a family of this size?" he asked jocosely.

"I fancy I feel much like the hen that hatched duck's eggs," Mrs. Clyde returned.

There was a laugh at this, in the midst of which Sarah Blake was heard to remark solemnly: "Yes, children are a great responsibility."

Whereat there was more laughter, and hardly had it subsided when from outside came the conductor's sonorous "All aboo —ard!"

"Girls, we're really going!" gasped Kitty.

There was a last vigorous waving of handkerchiefs out of the window. Suddenly a wail burst from Blue Bonnet: "Solomon! Solomon!"

All looked at one another aghast. In the excitement of the last moments no one had thought of the dog.

"Find Bennie Blake—he had Solomon last," cried Blue Bonnet, rushing to the platform.

"I'll find him, don't you worry," exclaimed Alec, swinging down the steps just as the first creaks of the car gave notice of starting.

"Alec—you'll get left!" cried Blue Bonnet. "There's Bennie, —oh, quick!"

Sure enough, there on the edge of the crowd was Bennie, but alack!—no Solomon.

"Stop the train, can't you, Uncle Cliff?" wailed Blue Bonnet. "Alec will be left—and Solomon too—"

Uncle Cliff leaped to the bottom step,—the train was still only crawling,—and with one hand on the rail leaned out and peered after Alec. Blue Bonnet gave a nervous clutch at his

C. E. Jacobs & Edyth Ellerbeck Read

sleeve. What he saw evidently reassured Mr. Ashe, for suddenly he straightened up and held out both arms. A second later a brown furry object came hurtling through the air and was caught ignominiously by the tail. Quick as a flash Uncle Cliff tossed the indignant Solomon to Blue Bonnet, and bent down to lend a helping hand to Alec. That young gentleman scrambled up with more haste than elegance, just as the train ceased to crawl and settled down to the real business of travelling.

"I'll never forget this, Alec Trent, as long as I live,—I think you deserve a Carnegie medal!" Blue Bonnet cried fervently. "I'd never get over it if Solomon should be lost."

"He wouldn't have been—lost, exactly," returned Alec in an odd tone.

"Why, what do you mean? Where did you find him?" Blue Bonnet demanded.

And Alec, bursting into a laugh in spite of his awful news, returned: "I found him just where that Blake boy left him— tied on to the end of the car!"

CHAPTER II

IN THE BLUE BONNET COUNTRY

"IF one of you speaks aloud in the next five minutes," declared Blue Bonnet earnestly, "I'll never forgive you."

No one being inclined to risk Blue Bonnet's undying enmity, there was complete silence for the space of time imposed. They were rolling along the smooth white road between the railway station and the ranch, Grandmother Clyde and the girls in a buckboard drawn by sturdy little mustangs, while Alec, Uncle Joe and Uncle Cliff, who had stayed behind to look after the luggage, were following on horseback.

Blue Bonnet sat tense and still, her hands clasped in her lap, the color coming and going in her face in rapid waves of pink and white; her eyes very shiny, her lips quivering. This home-coming was having an effect she had not dreamed of. Every familiar object, every turn of the road that brought her nearer the beloved ranch, gave her a new and delicious thrill.

As they neared the modern wire fence two dusky little greaser piccaninnies rose out of the chaparral, hurled themselves on the big gate and held it open, standing like sentinels, bursting with importance, as the buckboard rolled through.

C. E. Jacobs & Edyth Ellerbeck Read

"They're Pancho's twins!" cried Blue Bonnet. "Stop, Miguel, while I give them something." Hurriedly seizing a half-eaten box of candy from Amanda's surprised hands, Blue Bonnet leaned down and tossed it to the grinning youngsters.

"*Muchas gracias*, Senorita!" they cried in a duet, their black eyes wide with joy.

"Bless the babies!" exclaimed Kitty, "—did you hear what they called you?"

Blue Bonnet laughed. "I'm never called anything else here. They meant 'Many thanks, Ma'am.' You will be 'Senorita' too,—better get used to it."

"Oh, I shall love it," cried Kitty. "It sounds like a title—'my lady' or 'your grace' or something grand."

"Grandmother will be 'Senora'—doesn't it just suit her, girls?" asked Blue Bonnet.

"Mrs. Clyde, may we call you 'Senora,' too?" asked Debby, "—just while we're on the ranch?"

"Debby believes in the eternal fitness of things," put in Kitty.

"Certainly, you may call me Senora," said Mrs. Clyde. "When you're in Texas do as the Texans do," she paraphrased.

"I intend to learn all the Spanish I can while I'm here," remarked Sarah. "I brought a grammar and a dictionary—"

A chorus of indignation went up from the other girls.

"This isn't a 'General Culture Club,' Sarah Blake," scolded Kitty. "We didn't come to the Blue Bonnet ranch for mutual improvement—but for *fun*!"

"We'll make a bonfire of those books," warned Blue Bonnet.

"All the Spanish that I can absorb through my—pores, is welcome to stick," said Debby, "but I'm not going to dig for it."

Sarah tactfully changed the subject. "Your house is a good way from the gate, Blue Bonnet," she remarked.

"Nearly two miles," Blue Bonnet smiled.

"There's nothing like owning all outdoors!" commented Kitty.

"Grandfather used to own nearly all outdoors," returned Blue Bonnet. "When father was a little boy nobody had fences and the cattle ranged through two or three counties. But now we keep a lot of fence-riders, who don't do a thing but mend fences, day after day. There's the bridge,—now as soon as we cross the river you can see the ranch-house."

"Is this what you call the 'river?'" Sarah asked, as they rattled over the pretty little stream.

"We call it a 'rio' in Texas, and you'd better not insult us by calling it a creek, Senorita Blake," Blue Bonnet warned her.

"I won't—'rio' is such a pretty name," said Sarah, making a mental note of it for future use.

"There!" cried Blue Bonnet, "behold the 'casa' of the Blue Bonnet ranch!"

What they saw was a long, low, rambling house, with wide, hospitable verandas embowered in half-tropical vines. It had evidently started out as a one-roomed, Spanish 'adobe,' and, as the needs of the family demanded it, an ell had been added here, a room there, like cells in a bee-hive, until now it covered a good deal of territory, still keeping its one-storied, Mission-like character.

"Oh, Blue Bonnet—it's just what I wanted it to be," exclaimed Kitty. "It looks as if a fat, Spanish monk might come out of that door this very minute."

"Instead of which there is my dear old Benita, and Pancho and his wife and the children and—oh, everybody!" Blue Bonnet was bouncing up and down now with excitement.

Alec and the other two riders came up in a cloud of dust just as Miguel raced the mustangs up to the veranda steps, where all the ranch hands were gathered to greet the young Senorita.

"Senorita mia!" cried Benita, and Blue Bonnet leaped from the wheel straight into her old nurse's arms.

"And this is Grandmother, Benita," said Blue Bonnet, helping Mrs. Clyde from her place.

"The little Senora's mother—God bless you!" cried Benita in Spanish. Then, in spite of her stiff joints, she made a deep, old-fashioned curtsy.

Tears sprang to the eyes of the Eastern woman. "Thank you, Benita," she said. "My daughter always wrote lovingly of you."

"Blessed Senora!" breathed Benita fervently.

"This is my grandmother, everybody," said Blue Bonnet,

presenting Mrs. Clyde to the entire circle, "and these are my friends—'amigos' from Massachusetts."

"Pleased to know ye!" said Pinto Pete and Shady, the only American cowboys on the ranch; while the Mexicans, as one voice, gave a hearty chorus of greeting.

The six "amigos" from Massachusetts were thrilled to the core, although at the same time a trifle embarrassed as to the correct way of responding to this vociferous welcome. Blue Bonnet set them all an example: she had a smile and a word for every man, woman and child, and finally sent them all off with a—"Come back when my trunks arrive!" And the hint brought a fresh gleam to already beaming faces.

Later, after a bountiful supper, they all gathered once more on the broad veranda while Blue Bonnet distributed her gifts. That those days in New York had been profitably spent was fully attested now when the contents of the many trunks were displayed. There were ribbons, scarfs and gay beads for the women, toys and sweets for the children, and wonderful pocket-knives, pipes and tobacco pouches for the men.

The Blue Bonnet ranch had been part of an original Spanish land-grant in the days when Texas was still part of Mexico, and had descended from father to son until it came into the hands of Blue Bonnet's grandfather. Many of the Mexican ranch-hands had been born on the place and looked on the Ashe family as their natural guardians and protectors. As yet they had not acquired a Yankee sense of independence, nor had they lost the soft Southern courtesy inherent in their race. They came up one at a time to Blue Bonnet as she stood at the top of the steps, her gifts in a great heap beside her; and each one, as he received his gift from her hand, called down a blessing on the head of the young Senorita. Then, laughing, chatting, and comparing gifts like a crowd of

C. E. Jacobs & Edyth Ellerbeck Read

children, they trooped away, the single men to the "bunk-house" by the big corral, the married couples and their children to little cabins scattered over the place.

"It's just like some old Spanish tale," declared Alec. "Blue Bonnet is a princess just returned to her castle, and all the serfs are come to pay her homage."

"I suppose Don Quixote will be off soon, hunting wind-mills?" suggested Kitty, with a mocking glance at Alec, whose new gun was the pride of his heart.

Alec deigned no reply.

"Look!" said Mrs. Clyde, softly, "—there goes the sun."

They followed her glance across the prairie that stretched away, green and softly undulating, in front of the veranda, and watched the red disk as it sank in a blaze of glory at the edge of the plain.

"Now you know," said Blue Bonnet, "why I felt like pushing back the houses in Woodford—at first they just suffocated me."

Mrs. Clyde smiled with new understanding. "You probably agree with our Massachusetts writer who complained that people in cities live too close together and not near enough," she said, patting Blue Bonnet's head as the girl, sitting on the step below her, leaned against her knee.

"Didn't you ever get lonesome here?" asked Debby, snuggling up to Amanda. She had been brought up among houses.

"Lonesome?" echoed Blue Bonnet. "I never knew what

lonesome meant—till my first day in school!"

All too soon came bedtime.

"Where are we all to sleep?" Blue Bonnet asked Benita. It was like Blue Bonnet not to give the matter a thought until beds were actually in demand.

Benita led the way proudly. "The Senora will have the little Senora's room," she said, throwing open the door of that long unused chamber.

Mrs. Clyde entered it with softened eyes.

"Senorita's own room is ready for her, and here is place for the others." Benita proceeded to the very end of a long ell to a huge airy room, seemingly all windows. It was Blue Bonnet's old nursery, and, next to the living-room, the largest room in the house. Four single beds, one in each corner, showed how Benita had solved the sleeping problem.

The girls gave a shout of delight; visions of bedtime frolics and long talks after lights were out, sent them dancing about the place.

"I tell you what," announced Blue Bonnet, "—if you imagine I am going off by myself when there's a sleeping-party like this going on, you're mistaken. I say—" here she turned on Sarah, "—you've always wanted a bed-room all to yourself; you told me so, one day. Well, here's your chance—you're welcome to every inch of mine!"

Sarah, quite willing to confine her "parties" to daylight hours, accepted the proposition eagerly. Maybe then she could get a peek at those Spanish books.

C. E. Jacobs & Edyth Ellerbeck Read

"Are you sure you're willing to give it up?" she asked quite honestly.

And Blue Bonnet with an incredulous stare returned: "Are you quite willing to give *this* up?"

"Perfectly!" exclaimed Sarah with such promptness that Blue Bonnet dismissed her lurking suspicion that Sarah was just "being polite" and accepted the exchange.

It was a happy Sarah who tucked herself away in a little bed all to herself, in a dainty room destined to be her very own for two long months. Four times happy was the quartet who shared the nursery. It was a long time before they subsided. There were so many things to be observed and discussed in that delightful place. Uncle Joe Terry had had a hand in its arrangement, and now that worthy man would have felt well repaid if he could have heard the gales of merriment over his masterpieces of interior decoration.

In her childhood Blue Bonnet had been blessed—or afflicted—with more dolls than ever fell to the lot of child before. Now the long-discarded nursery-folk formed a frieze around the entire room, the poor darlings being, like Blue-beard's wives, suspended by their hair. Every nationality and every degree of mutilation was there represented, and the effect was funny beyond description. On the broad mantel-shelf over the stone fireplace reposed drums, merry-go-rounds, trumpets and toy horses; while on the hearth was a tiny kitchen range bearing a complete assortment of pots and pans of a most diminutive size. In every available nook of the room stood doll-carriages, rocking-horses, go-carts and fire-engines, each showing the scars of Blue Bonnet's stormy childhood.

"I wish," cried Kitty, "that we weren't any of us a day over seven!"

While the girls were still making merry over her childhood treasures Blue Bonnet slipped away. She had not had a word alone with Uncle Cliff for days, and had exchanged only a hurried greeting with Uncle Joe at the station. And there were such heaps of things to talk over!

She found them both on the veranda, enjoying the evening breeze that came laden with sweet scents from off the prairie. Blue Bonnet clapped her hands over Uncle Joe's eyes in her old madcap fashion.

"It's Blue Bon—er—Elizabeth, I mean," he guessed promptly.

"Wrong!" cried Blue Bonnet sternly. "Elizabeth Ashe was left behind in Massachusetts, and only Blue Bonnet has come back to the ranch."

"Thank goodness for that!" breathed Uncle Joe devoutly. "Elizabeth came mighty hard. It didn't fit, somehow. I reckon you're glad to get *home*, Blue Bonnet?"

"Glad? Why, there isn't a word in the whole English dictionary that means just what I feel, Uncle Joe," replied Blue Bonnet, perching on the arm of his chair. "I love every inch of the state of Texas."

The two men exchanged a significant glance that was not lost on Blue Bonnet.

"Oh, I know what you are thinking of, Uncle Cliff. You remember the day when I said I hated the West and all it stood for. I meant that too—then. But I feel different now. It isn't that I'm sorry I went away; I just had to go, feeling as I did. I reckon I'll always be that way—I have to find things out for myself."

Uncle Joe smiled humorously. "Reckon we're most of us built that way, eh, Cliff?"

Mr. Ashe gave a rueful nod. "Yes, what the other fellow has been through doesn't count for much. We all have to blister our fingers before we'll believe that fire really burns."

They were all silent for a moment.

"Has any one seen Solomon?" asked Blue Bonnet suddenly.

"I think Don is showing him over the ranch," replied Uncle Joe. "I saw them both headed for the stables a while ago."

"I'm glad they're going to get on well," said Blue Bonnet in a relieved tone. "I was afraid Don would be jealous." She gave a clear loud whistle, and a moment later the two animals came racing across the yard, tumbling over each other in their eagerness to be first up the steps. Blue Bonnet stooped and picked up the smaller dog, fondling him and saying foolish things. Don, the big collie, gave a low whine and looked up at her piteously.

"Not jealous, did you say?" laughed Uncle Joe.

Blue Bonnet patted the collie's head. "Good dog," she said soothingly. "You're too big to be carried, Don." Then she put down Solomon and bending put a hand under Don's muzzle; his soft eyes met hers affectionately. "I'm going to put Solomon in your charge—understand? You must warn him about snakes, Don,—and don't let the coyotes get him." A sharp bark from Don Blue Bonnet was satisfied to take for an affirmative answer, and with another pat sent him off for the night.

"Has Alec some place to sleep?" inquired Blue Bonnet, her hospitable instincts suddenly and rather tardily aroused.

"Benita has put him in the ell by me. He's there now, unpacking to-night so that he won't have to waste any time to-morrow. I never saw a boy so keen about ranch-life as he is. He seems to look on himself as a sort of pioneer in a new country," Uncle Joe chuckled.

"It's all new to him," rejoined Blue Bonnet. "This is his first glimpse of the West. I hope he gets strong and well out here—General Trent worries so about him."

"It will be the making of him," Uncle Cliff assured her. "He'll go back to Massachusetts as husky as Pinto Pete, if he'll just learn to live outdoors, and leave books alone for a while."

"I'm going to hide every book he has brought with him," declared Blue Bonnet. "And Sarah Blake will need looking after—she has the book habit, too."

Uncle Joe shook his head. "It seems to be a germ disease they have back there in Massachusetts. Glad you didn't catch it, Blue Bonnet."

"Oh, I'm immune!" laughed she, as she said good-night and went to seek Benita.

She found her old nurse in the kitchen, resting after an arduous day. Gertrudis, the famous cook "loaned" for the summer by a neighboring ranch, was mixing something mysterious in a wooden bowl, while her granddaughter Juanita, a nut-brown beauty, pirouetted about the room, showing off her new rosettes in a Spanish dance.

Blue Bonnet clapped her hands. "That's a pretty step, Juanita,—will you teach it to me some day?"

"Si, Senorita," she assented eagerly, showing all her white teeth in a delighted smile. "It is the *cachucha*."

"The girls will all want to learn it," Blue Bonnet assured her. She draw Benita into the dining-room and then gave her a hearty squeeze. "Everything's just lovely, you old dear," she cried. "The girls are crazy about the nursery, and they think you are the dearest ever!"

Benita's wrinkled face beamed. "If the Senorita is pleased, old Benita is happy," she said deprecatingly.

"Benita, I missed you dreadfully, off there in Woodford. I had to make my own bed and do my own mending!"

Benita gave an odd little sound of distress. "But Benita will do it now," she urged anxiously.

"You'll have to get around Grandmother then, Benita,—I can't."

"The Senora is kind—" Benita began.

"—but firm," added Blue Bonnet. "I leave her to you!"

It was so late before the girls finally settled down into their respective corners, that it seemed only about five minutes before they were awakened at daybreak by the most terrific tumult that ever smote the ears of slumbering innocence.

Bang, bang! Boom, crash, bang! Shouts, yells, wild Comanche-like cries rent the ear, and punctuated the incessant booming that shook even the thick adobe walls of the nursery.

Four terrified faces were raised simultaneously from four white beds, and four voices in chorus whispered: "What is it?" No one dared stir.

Suddenly the door was burst open and in sprang a white-robed figure, hair flying, eyes wide with terror. Straight to Blue Bonnet's bed the spectre flew and leaped into the middle of it with a plump that made its occupant gasp.

"Oh, girls, it's Indians!" wailed the newcomer; and then they saw that it was Sarah.

"Indians?" exclaimed Blue Bonnet. "There aren't any Indians around here. Get off my chest and I'll go see."

Casting off the bed-clothes and the startled Sarah at the same time, with one spring Blue Bonnet was at the window. What she saw there was hardly reassuring; the whole space between the house and the stables seemed to be filled with a howling, whirling mass of men. In the gray half-light of early dawn she could recognize no one. Suddenly a fresh explosion set the windows rattling; there was a hiss and a glare of red. In the glow she caught a glimpse of Alec; he held a revolver and was shooting it with sickening rapidity, not stopping to take aim.

Blue Bonnet staggered back faint with horror, and the girls gathered fearfully about her. Uncle Cliff's voice giving an order came to them from outside. Blue Bonnet leaned out and shrieked—"Uncle, Uncle—what's the matter—oh, what is it?"

Never had voice seemed so welcome as those calm, soothing tones, when Uncle Cliff replied: "Reckon you've forgotten what day it is, Honey."

Blue Bonnet turned on the girls. "What—what day is it?"

And the light from within was suddenly greater than that from without as they answered in a sheepish chorus:

"The Fourth of July!"

CHAPTER III

THE GLORIOUS FOURTH

"TO think that a crowd of New England girls, of all people, should forget the Fourth of July!" exclaimed Alec, when they met around the big breakfast table, later that morning.

Sarah looked positively pained. "I never forgot it before in my whole life," she said plaintively. "But there have been so many new things to think of, and travelling, you know—" she ended lamely.

"Are New England people supposed to be more patriotic than those of other states?" inquired Blue Bonnet, bristling a little in defence of Texas.

"Certainly!" cried Alec. "New England folks are fed on Plymouth Rock and the Declaration of Independence from the cradle to the grave. That's the diet of patriots."

"H'm!" murmured Blue Bonnet scornfully. "I'll wager that Patriot Alec Trent would have forgotten Independence Day, too, if Uncle Cliff hadn't let him into the secret. Now I know, Uncle Cliff, what was in that box labelled 'dangerous.' Wasn't I a goose not to think of it? And Uncle Joe telegraphed so as to get us here in time. Grandmother," here she

C. E. Jacobs & Edyth Ellerbeck Read

turned a rueful countenance on Mrs. Clyde, "going to school hasn't helped my head a bit, I'm just downright *dull*."

Uncle Cliff gave an amused laugh. "I'm glad to have caught you napping for once, young lady. Now, as soon as Gertrudis stops sending in corncake, I propose that we adjourn to the stables and look over the mounts. Pinto Pete says he has a nice little bunch of ponies."

"Why do they call him 'Pinto?'" asked Debby. "I thought that meant a spotted horse."

"Haven't you noticed Pete's freckles?" asked Uncle Joe. "He has more and bigger ones than any other human in Texas, and the boys called him 'Pinto Pete' the first minute they clapped eyes on him. He don't mind—it's the way of the West."

"And is 'Shady' a nickname, too?" Debby asked.

"No—just short for good old-fashioned Shadrach. Shadrach Stringer's his name, and he's the best twister in the county."

Debby had a third question on her lips but checked it as she met Kitty's saucy eye. Kitty, known as "Little Miss Why," was always on the alert to bequeath the name to a successor. But Sarah saw none of the by-play and asked at once:

"What's a 'twister?'"

"A bronco buster," replied Uncle Joe.

Sarah's look of mystification at this definition sent Alec off into a fit of laughter. Blue Bonnet came to the rescue. "A twister breaks in the wild horses, Sarah. Some day we'll get him to give an exhibition. You'd never believe how he can stick on,—it'll frighten you the first time you see it. The way the horse rears and bucks and runs, why—" Blue Bonnet suddenly choked and turned pale. Mrs. Clyde and Uncle Cliff read her thoughts at the same moment and both rose hurriedly.

"Come on, everybody," exclaimed Mr. Ashe in a resolutely cheerful tone, "we must make the most of the morning."

"Why?" asked Kitty before she thought, and then bit her lip. That word "why" was such a pitfall.

"Everybody has to take a siesta in the afternoon," explained Blue Bonnet. "It's too hot to move."

"Every afternoon?" demanded Debby.

"Every afternoon," repeated Uncle Cliff. "Anybody caught awake between one and four P. M. will be severely dealt with. It's a law of the human constitution and the penalty is imprisonment in the hospital, headache, and loss of appetite."

"What a waste of time," Sarah commented, privately resolving that she would not spend two or three precious hours every afternoon in sleep. One didn't come to Texas every summer.

"I see mutiny in Sarah's eye," said Blue Bonnet. "Wait till you've had a sunstroke, Sarah, then you'll wish you hadn't possessed such oceans of energy." She had put all unpleasant memories from her by now and was leading the way to the stables. Straight to Firefly's stall she went and threw her arms around her old playfellow's neck. In the few seconds before the others came in she had whispered into his velvet ear something that was both a confession and an apology, while Firefly nosed her softly and looked as pleased as a mere horse-countenance is capable of looking.

"Isn't he a beauty?" she challenged as the rest entered.

"A stunner," Alec agreed warmly, coming up to admire. "Wouldn't Chula's nose be out of joint if she could see you petting Firefly?"

"Victor has a rival too. Where's Alec's horse, Uncle Joe?"

Pinto Pete came up just then, his freckles seeming to the girls to loom up larger and browner than ever now that they knew the origin of his nickname. "Shady says the roan's too skittish for any of the young ladies—" he suggested.

"Strawberry?—oh, she's splendid! Alec, you'll think you're in a cradle."

The pretty creature, just the color of her namesake, was brought out and put through her paces, and the exhibition proved to the satisfaction of all the young ladies that Shady's verdict was quite just. Strawberry pranced, bared her teeth at any approach, and in general did her best to live up to her reputation for skittishness. The fighting blood in Alec made him resolve to change that adjective to "kittenish" before he had ridden her many times.

The four ponies provided for the girls were next brought out for inspection, and met with unqualified approval from all but Sarah. These slender, restless little steeds seemed not at all related to the fat placid beasts to which she had heretofore trusted herself. Her face betokened her unspoken dismay.

"Sallikins, I know the best mount for you," exclaimed Kitty innocently.

"Oh, do you?" cried Sarah hopefully.

"Um-hum,—Blue Bonnet's old rocking-horse in the nursery!" laughed Kitty; whereupon Pinto Pete let out a loud guffaw, changing it at once into an ostentatious fit of coughing when he saw that Sarah was inclined to resent Kitty's insult.

Her mild blue eyes almost flashed as she returned: "You can pick out any one of those four horses you choose for me, Kitty Clark, and I'll show you if I'm afraid to ride!"

This outburst from Sarah the placid rather startled the We are Sevens. But Kitty, after a surprised stare at the ruffled one, picked up the gauntlet. She appraised the horses with a calculating glance, then picked out a chestnut who showed the whites of his eyes in a most terrifying manner.

"How does that one suit you, Senorita Blake?" she asked tauntingly.

"Very well," returned Sarah with a toss of her flaxen braids. This was sheer bravado, but it passed muster. No one dreamed of the shivers of abject fear that were chasing up and down the girl's spine at sight of the fiery little chestnut with the awful eyes.

"Why, that's Comanche!" exclaimed Blue Bonnet. "He has a heavenly gait."

"Comanche!" Alec echoed, and then withdrew hastily to a convenient stall. The thought of the plump, blond Sarah mounted on a steed bearing such a wild Indian name was too much for him. He emerged a moment later very red in the face and unable to meet Blue Bonnet's eye. Their sense of humor was curiously akin, and Blue Bonnet knew, without

C. E. Jacobs & Edyth Ellerbeck Read

being told, what mental picture filled Alec's mind.

"Why not have a ride this morning,—there's plenty of time before noon," suggested Uncle Joe. "Here, Lupe, bring out the saddles," he called.

Guadalupe, the "wrangler," appeared from an inner room, looking like a chief of the Navajo tribe, so burdened was he with the bright-hued Indian saddle-blankets. The girls watched him with eager eyes, but when he was followed by several boys bearing huge cowboy saddles, there was a little murmur of dismay from the group.

"Men's saddles for us!" exclaimed Debby in a shocked undertone.

Blue Bonnet laughed outright. "Didn't you hear Grandmother say: 'When you're in Texas do as the Texans do?' Well, turn and turn about is fair play. Didn't I ride a side-saddle as proper as pie in Woodford? Now it's your turn."

Sarah gave an approving look at the high pommels of the saddles, and at the strong hair-bridle that was being fitted over Comanche's wicked little head.

Blue Bonnet gave the same bridle a look that was far from approving. "Lupe, isn't that a Spanish bit you're using?"

"Si, Senorita," said Guadalupe guiltily.

"Then take it right off!" commanded Blue Bonnet in her old imperious way. "They're cruel wicked things that cut a horse's mouth to pieces, and I won't have them used," she explained to the girls. "Lupe knows I hate them." She turned accusingly on the boy.

Lupe looked at her appealingly. "It is the safer for the Senoritas," he urged.

Blue Bonnet was inexorable. "We're not going to do any lassoing or branding, Lupe, and can manage very well without them. We'll have to organize a humane society, girls, and reform these cruel cowmen," she suggested.

Lupe discarded the offending bits and substituted others more to the Senorita's liking, and then the girls went in to dress for the ride.

"How can we ride across the saddle in these skirts?" demanded Debby.

Blue Bonnet and Uncle Cliff exchanged a significant glance, the reason for which was explained a moment later when the girls entered the nursery. There on the beds lay five complete riding suits: divided skirts of khaki, "middy" blouses of a cooler material, and soft Panama hats, each wound with a blue scarf and finished with a smart bow.

"How darling of you!" cried the girls, falling on Blue Bonnet rapturously.

"It's all Uncle Cliff," exclaimed Blue Bonnet. "He saw some suits like these in a shop window while we were in New York and went in and ordered seven! But Susy and Ruth won't have a chance to wear theirs," she ended regretfully.

The girls, too excited to spend time mourning the absent ones, were already getting into the fascinating suits. These were all of a size, close lines not being demanded of a middy blouse, and all were pronounced perfect except Sarah's, which, as Kitty remarked, "fitted too soon." Gauntlet gloves and natty riding whips completed the equipment of the

C. E. Jacobs & Edyth Ellerbeck Read

riders, and when they went out ready to mount they were as neat a crowd of equestriennes as ever graced Central Park.

Notwithstanding that they were all dressed alike, each girl's particular type stood out quite clearly. Kitty had more "style" than the other Woodford girls, and a carriage that had more of conscious vanity in it; her "middy" set more trimly and the little hat was set on her ruddy locks at a little more daring angle than that of the others. Amanda and Debby appeared the same unremarkable sort of schoolgirls that they always were. The costume was not designed for maidens of Sarah's build, and it looked quite as uncomfortable on her as she felt in it. Blue Bonnet appeared as she always did in this sort of attire: as though it had grown on her.

"Whew!" exclaimed Alec, "such elegance!"

"Strikes me you're not so slow yourself," returned Kitty. "Isn't he 'got up regardless,' girls?"

Alec was dressed for his part with elaborate attention to details. Mr. Ashe had been anxiously consulted, for the Eastern boy had no desire to be dubbed a tenderfoot; and now, except for its spotless newness, his costume was quite "Western and ranchified"—according to Blue Bonnet.

He was in khaki, too, with trousers that tucked into high "puttees"—thick pigskin leggings which gave his long limbs quite a substantial appearance and himself no end of comfort. A soft shirt and a carelessly knotted bandana gave the finishing touches to his attire. He had even turned in the neck of his shirt so as to be quite one of the cowmen, secretly hoping that the girls would not notice how white his throat was.

It was a gay cavalcade that cantered out of the big corral, the five girls leading; Alec, Pinto Pete, and Uncle Joe forming a rear guard, with Don and Solomon capering at their heels; while a crowd of little "greasers" clung on to the bars, their eyes big with the wonder of it all.

"Lucky we're not on the streets of Woodford," remarked Alec, looking with amused eyes over the well mounted company.

"Why?" asked Blue Bonnet a trifle resentfully. "Aren't we grand enough for the East?"

"Sure! But I'm afraid we'd be arrested for running a circus without a license!"

This piece of wit so tickled Pinto Pete that he nearly stampeded the bunch by bursting again into his ear-splitting laugh. Sarah grabbed the handy pommel with a nervous clutch that was eloquent of her state of mind. And that action was all that saved her. For Comanche, taking Pete's guffaw for a command, leaped forward like a cat, and a moment later the whole crowd was galloping madly across the level meadow.

It is probable that if Sarah's hair had not already been as light as hair can well be, that wild ride would have turned it several shades lighter. The terrors that were compressed into those two hours are beyond description, while the bobbing, bumping and shaking of her poor plump body left reminders that only time and witch hazel were able to eradicate.

When they returned at noon Gertrudis had a wonderful dinner awaiting them, and the riders, with their appetites freshened by the air and exercise, fell upon it like a pack of famished wolves. All except Sarah. Protesting that she was not in the least hungry, she went at once to her room. On the little stand by her bed lay the Spanish grammar and dictionary, mute evidences of the way she had intended to spend the siesta hour. She gave them not so much as a glance, but stepping out of her clothes left them in a heap where they fell,—an action indicating a state of demoralization hardly to be believed of the parson's daughter,—and flung herself into bed with a groan.

Two hours later she was awakened by the other four girls who had turned inquisitors, and while two were stripping off the bedclothes the other two applied a feather to the soles of her feet.

"Oh—is it morning?" gasped Sarah, sitting up and rubbing her eyes. "It doesn't seem as if I had been asleep a minute."

"Such a waste of time!" quoted Kitty mockingly. "There's such a thing, Sarah, as overdoing the siesta," she taunted.

Sarah drew up her feet and sat on them, smothering the groan that arose to her lips at the action. Every bone and joint had a new and awful kind of ache, and in that minute Sarah wished she had never heard of the Blue Bonnet ranch. Just then came the welcome clatter of dishes and at the doorway appeared Benita bearing a tray of good things, while back of her was Grandmother Clyde.

"Now off with you,—you tormentors," the Senora commanded gaily. "This poor child must be nearly famished."

"Grandmother's pet!" sang Blue Bonnet over her shoulder, as obeying orders, the four girls left the suffering Sarah in peace.

Existence assumed a brighter hue to Sarah when she had eaten the generous repast Benita set before her; and when she had bathed and rubbed herself with the Pond's Extract Mrs. Clyde had secretly provided her with, life seemed once more worth living. But she was very quiet and moved with great circumspection for the rest of the day, quite content to leave to the others the handling of the fireworks in the evening.

Uncle Cliff's "dangerous" box yielded still more wonders. The noisy bombs and giant crackers of the morning were followed by pyrotechnics that aroused unbounded admiration from the grown-ups and caused an excitement among the small greasers that threatened to end in a human conflagration. A small fortune went up in gigantic pin-wheels; flower-pots that sent up amazing blossoms in all the hues of the rainbow; rockets that burst in mid-air and let fall a shower of coiling snakes, which, in their turn, exploded into a myriad stars; Roman candles that sometimes went off at the wrong end and caused a wild scattering of the audience in their immediate vicinity; and "set-pieces" that were the epitome of this school of art.

It would have been hard to say which was most tired, the hostess or her guests, when the last spark faded from the big "Lone Star" of Texas which ended the show. No bedtime frolic to-night; the four in the nursery undressed in a dead quiet and fell asleep before their heads fairly touched the pillows. In her own little room Sarah held another seance with the witch hazel bottle, and went to sleep only to dream of a wild ride across the meadows on Blue Bonnet's rocking-horse, with a fierce band of Comanche Indians pursuing her, yelling fiendishly all the while, and keeping up a mad fusillade of Roman candles.

CHAPTER IV

THE ROUND ROBIN

"WHAT'S the program for this morning?" asked Uncle Cliff, as the ranch party assembled on the veranda after a very late breakfast.

"I don't know what the others are going to do," said Sarah, "but I'm going to write letters."

The other girls exchanged amused glances: it was evident that Sarah wished to forestall suggestions of another ride. Kitty was beginning to show symptoms of sauciness when Mrs. Clyde interrupted kindly with—"I think Sarah's suggestion quite in order. Every one at home will be looking for letters."

"Uncle Cliff telegraphed," said Blue Bonnet, loath to settle down to so prosaic a pursuit.

"But a telegram isn't very satisfying to mothers and fathers, dear," replied her grandmother. "And think of poor Susy and Ruth."

"I intend to write them, too," remarked Sarah.

"Let's all write them!" exclaimed Blue Bonnet.

"That's the right spirit," said Senora with an approving nod. "A 'round-robin' letter will cheer the poor girls wonderfully."

"You hear the motion, are all in favor?" asked Alec.

"Will you write a 'robin,' too?" bargained Kitty, who loved to torment the youth.

"Sure!" he agreed at once, thus taking the wind out of her sails.

"Aye, aye, then!" they all exclaimed, and the motion was declared carried.

There was a scattering for paper and ink, after which every one settled down for an hour's scribbling, some using the broad rail of the veranda as a table, others repairing to desks in the house. Blue Bonnet doubled up jack-knife fashion on one of the front steps, using her knees for a pad; while Sarah, complaining that she could not think with so many people about her, took herself off to the window-seat in the nursery.

"The idea of wanting to think!" exclaimed Kitty. "I never stop to think when I write letters."

"You don't need to tell that to any one who has ever heard from you," remarked Blue Bonnet. "The one letter I had from you in New York took me an hour to puzzle out,—it began in the middle and ended at the top of the first page, and there were six 'ands' and four 'ifs' in one sentence."

"That's quite an accomplishment—I'll wager you couldn't get in half so many," retorted Kitty. And then for a while there was silence, broken only by the scratching of pens and the query from Blue Bonnet as to whether there were two s's or two p's in "disappoint."

"TO SUSY AND RUTH DOYLE, WOODFORD, MASSACHUSETTS.
"THE BLUE BONNET RANCH,
"July the fifth.

"YOU POOR DEARS: You'll never know if you live to be a thousand years old what a fearful disappointment it was when Doctor Clark told me the awful news. Where did you get it? Is it very bad? And do you have to gargle peroxide of hydrogen? Amanda says she just lived on it when her throat was bad. Are you honestly as red as lobsters? It's a perfect shame you should have to be sick—and in vacation, too. There might be some advantages if it should happen—say at examination time. Grandmother says it is very unusual to have scarlet fever in warm weather,—it just seems as if you must have gone out of your way to get it—or it went out of its way to get you.

"The ranch party isn't a bit complete without you. I'm going to take pictures of everything and everybody so as to show you when we get back. That sounds as if I meant to go back again next fall, when really it isn't decided yet. I'm more in love with the ranch than ever and feel as if I never wanted to leave it again. It's so fine and big out here. There's so much air to breathe and such a long way to look, and you can throw a stone as far as you like without 'breaking a window or a tradition'—as Alec says. We have our traditions, too, but they can stand any amount of stone-throwing—in fact that's part of them.

"It's worth crossing the continent to see Sarah on horseback, riding across the saddle in a wild Western way that would shock her reverend father out of a whole paragraph. Kitty dared her and I must say she showed pluck—Comanche can go *some* when he gets started, and Sarah stayed with him to the finish. But you can imagine why she wanted to write letters to-day instead of riding again. You can thank her for the round robin. There, I've reached the bottom of the page before I've begun to tell you anything. But the others will make up for it, I reckon. No more now—I must save strength for a letter to Aunt Lucinda. Do hurry and get well and out of quarantine so that you can write to

"Your devoted
"BLUE BONNET."

"DEAR SUSY AND RUTH: We arrived on Monday evening after a very pleasant journey. The name of the station where you get off is Jonah—isn't that odd? We had to drive twenty miles in a very queer kind of vehicle in order to reach Blue Bonnet's home, and this letter will have to go back over the same road in order to be posted. I think I had better go back to the beginning and tell you all about our trip from the time we left Woodford.

"The private car we came in is called The Wanderer and it is really a pity you could not have shared it with us. It is much grander than Mrs. Clyde's drawing-room at home,—the mahogany shone till you could see your face in it, and wherever there was not mahogany there was a mirror, and Slivers, the porter, dusted everything about twenty times a day. If you could see Slivers I should not have to explain why he is called by that name. I am sure he is the tallest and slimmest man I have ever seen. And that is odd, too, for you always think of them as plump and fat. He is a negro, you know, and doesn't seem to mind it a bit, but is as jolly as if he were white and as fat as you think he ought to be, and sang and played his banjo

C. E. Jacobs & Edyth Ellerbeck Read

in the evenings quite like a civilized person. He waited on table, too, while the chief—the cook, you know—prepared our meals in the most cunning little kitchen you can imagine.

"It was a very interesting trip. Sometimes we would begin our breakfast in one state and before we had finished we would be in another, and yet there would seem to be no difference. I think travelling is a very interesting way to learn Geography, for you forget to think of Kansas as yellow and Oklahoma as purple, and think of them as *real* places with trees and farms and other things like Massachusetts. I knew already that Texas is as big as all the New England states put together, but I never really *grasped* it before. I am learning new things every day, some Spanish, though not as much as I could wish. Yesterday I learned to ride astride. That is, nearly learned. I don't feel entirely at home that way yet and it has tired me considerably, but I dare say it will come easier after a while. My horse is named Comanche, and he looks just that way. There is more white to his eyes than anything else.

"Benita is Blue Bonnet's old nurse. She does the most exquisite drawn-work and is going to teach me (it would be as well for you not to mention this when you write) the spider-web stitch and the Maltese cross, so that I can do a waist for Blue Bonnet. She is doing so much for us all that I want to make some return for her hospitality. Blue Bonnet, I mean, not Benita.

"I do hope you will soon be better. I felt so mean at leaving without even saying good-bye. But I had to think of all my brothers and sisters and the girls—I couldn't expose them to the fever, you know. I hope you liked the postals we sent. Amanda and I came very near being left once when we couldn't find the post-box at Kansas City,—we had to run a block, while Alec and Kitty stood on the back platform and laid bets on the winner. (Amanda won.)

"We are all well and hope you are the same,—I mean I hope you are better and will soon be well.

"With best love,
"SARAH JANE BLAKE."

"Oh, girls, I am simply speechless and can't find a word to say when I try to describe our grand trip and this perfect peach of a place, and the glorious time we have had and are having ever since we left pokey old Woodford and arrived at the Blue Bonnet ranch. I keep pinching myself to see if I'm really me, but it isn't at all convincing, and I suppose I'll simply go on treading air and not believe in the reality of a thing till I come to earth in time to hear the Jolly Good say—'Miss Kitty, you may take problem number ninety-four'—and wake up to the monotonous old grind again—oh, if you could only see this darling old house and the picturesque Mexicans—rather dirty some of them (I suppose that's why they are called greasers) and the perfectly dear way they adore Blue Bonnet and their deference to her 'amigos'—I tell you I feel like a princess when they call me 'Senorita' with a musical accent that makes you downright sick with envy. Why anybody on earth ever left the West to go and settle up the East I don't see,—you may think I mean that the other way about but I don't, for anybody can see at half a glance that this country is as old as Methusalem—the live-oaks look as if they'd been here forever and ever and would stay as much longer—they're all 'hoary with moss' and all that sort of thing like that poem of Tennyson's—or maybe it is Longfellow's—it doesn't matter which in vacation, thank goodness. I don't like to seem to be rubbing it in about our good times, for it's just too hateful that you can't be here, too, and ride like mad for miles without coming to a fence and wear the adorable riding-suits Mr. Ashe got for us in New York—all seven alike and as becoming as anything—and have the best things to eat, wear, do, and see every minute of the day.

"This won't go into the envelope with the rest if I run on any longer so I'll close,—with a fat hard hug and lots of love to you both,

"KITTY."

"DEAR GIRLS: Don't you ever go and get conditioned at school; take my solemn warning. That awful thing hanging over me is going to do its best to spoil my grand summer in Texas. I intended to do a lot of studying as soon as we arrived here, so that I might have a few weeks perfectly free from worry; but goodness me, how can anybody open a book when there's something going on every blessed minute of the day? It's a pity it wasn't Sarah who was conditioned. She actually likes to study and if it came to a choice between a horseback ride and doing ten pages of grammar, she'd jump at the grammar. Sometimes I think Sarah isn't made like other girls. Not quite normal, you know.

"Now that I've seen Blue Bonnet at home, I realize what a hard time she must have had in Woodford, at first especially. She's treated like a perfect *queen* here, and doesn't have to mind a soul except Senora—that's what we call Mrs. Clyde. Fancy having run the ranch all your life and then at fifteen having to start in and obey Miss Clyde, and Mr. Hunt, and the rest of those mighty ones! I think she's a brick to have done it at all, and I take back every criticism I ever made of her. She must be terribly rich, but doesn't put on any airs at all.

"How is little old Woodford getting along without us? I'm almost ashamed to write Mother and Father, for I can't say I'm homesick and parents always expect you to be. Debby wants to finish my page, so no more now from

"Your loving AMANDA."

"DEAR SUSY AND RUTH: There's only room for me to say hello, and how are you? I wish I were a grand descriptive genius like Robert Louis Stevenson so that I could describe this wonderful Texas. But description isn't my strong point—you know how I just scraped through Eng. Comp. so I'll not try any flights.

"It isn't half as *wild* as we used to imagine it. The cowboys don't go shooting up towns and hanging horse-thieves to all the trees the way they do in most of the Western stories. Even the cattle are tame, but Blue Bonnet says that is because they are fenced nowadays, and most of them de-horned. All the cowboys except two are Mexicans, and they are so picturesque and—different. Mr. Ashe says Texas is filling up with negroes but he won't have any on the ranch,—he sticks to the Mexicans, and I'm mighty glad, for they seem just to suit the atmosphere. Juanita, who waits on the table, is a beauty, with the most coquettish airs. Miguel is in love with her, and we all hope she won't keep him waiting too long, for if they are really going to be married, we want a grand wedding while we are here. Wouldn't that be thrilling?

"I've just room to sign my name,

"Yours, with love,

C. E. Jacobs & Edyth Ellerbeck Read

"DEBBY."

"TO THE ABSENT TWO-SEVENTHS OF THE 'WE-ARE-ITS'—Greeting! Please don't imagine that I forced my way into this Round Robin affair. My masculine chirography probably looks out of place in this epistolary triumph—ahem!—but you can thank Kitty Clark for it. I don't know whether or not this is intended as a letter of condolence, but it surely ought to be,—anybody who has to miss this summer-session on the Blue Bonnet ranch deserves flowers and slow music.

"This letter will be postmarked 'Jonah'—but don't be alarmed; they say it's a harmless one. I'm going to ride over with the mail. Just a little matter of twenty miles, a trifle out here! Kitty says she doesn't see how we can expect any letters to reach a place with such a name, but I've faith in the collection of relatives left behind in Woodford.

"Now I advise you both, the next time you go into the vicinity of anything catching, cross your fingers and say 'King's Ex.' for you're missing the time of your young lives. As a place of residence, Texas certainly has my vote. A fellow can breathe his lungs full here without robbing the next fellow of oxygen.

"With unbounded sympathy,
"Yours,
"ALEC TRENT."

Blue Bonnet collected the literary installments from each of the different authors and put them in a big envelope.

"This 'round-robin' is as plump as a partridge," she remarked, "I hope Susy and Ruth won't strain their eyes devouring it."

"The Woodford postman in our part of town will have an unusually warm greeting, I fancy," said Mrs. Clyde, gathering up all the other letters and placing them with the round-robin in the roomy mail-bag.

"I think Father had better have a social at the church for the We-are-Seven relatives and ask them to bring our letters. Reading and passing them around would make a very interesting evening's entertainment," said Sarah.

Blue Bonnet paused long enough to shake her. "Don't you dare suggest such a horrible thing to your father, Sarah! My letter wasn't intended for—public consumption."

"Nor mine!" exclaimed Kitty. "Father and mother know what a scatter-brain I am, but it's a family skeleton which they don't care to have aired."

"Is the mail all in?" asked Alec in an official tone.

"All in, postmaster," replied Mrs. Clyde, fastening the bag and handing it to him with a smile. "You're not going alone, are you?"

"No, Shady is going along this trip, Senora," he replied.

"Why don't we all go?" asked Blue Bonnet; "it isn't much of a ride."

Sarah looked up in alarm, but met Mrs. Clyde's reassuring glance. "Not this time, dear," she returned to Blue Bonnet. "So far you have had all play and no work. The piano hasn't been touched since we arrived."

Blue Bonnet said nothing, but into her eyes there sprang a sudden rebellion. Out there by the stables Don and Solomon were frolicking, ready at a moment's notice to dash away at Firefly's heels. Away in front of the house stretched the road and the prairie, calling irresistibly to her restless, roving spirit. And vacation had been so long in coming! If grandmother were going to be like Aunt Lucinda—Again there flashed into her mind the wish so often voiced in Woodford: that there might be two of her, so that one might stay at home and be taught things while the other went wandering about as she liked. All at once she remembered Alec's suggestion—that she adopt Sarah as her "alter ego." A smile drove the cloud from her eyes. "Can't Sarah do my practising while I do her riding?" she asked coaxingly.

Her grandmother hid a smile as she said: "I was under the impression that my coming to the ranch was to see that Blue Bonnet Ashe did her practising, mending, and had coffee only on Sundays."

Blue Bonnet colored. She had uttered those very words, and nobody should say that an Ashe was not sincere. Straightening up she met the questioning looks of the other girls with a resolute glance. "Grandmother is right, as she always is, girls. I'll go and practise, and you—what will you do?"

"I'm sure all the girls will be glad of a little time to themselves," said the Senora. "Let us all do as we like until dinner-time. I've been longing to sit in the shade of the big magnolia ever since I came. I shall take a book and spend my two hours out there, and any one who wishes may share my bower."

"Then I'll be off," said Alec. "Any commissions for me in Jonah?" He stood like an orderly at attention, with the mail-bag slung over one shoulder and his whole bearing expressive of the importance of his mission. The sun and the wind of the prairie had already tanned his smooth skin to the ruddy hue of health, but Mrs. Clyde, observing him closely, could not fail to note how very slim and frail the erect young figure was.

"Isn't twenty miles a rather long ride on a hot day?" she asked tactfully, fearing to wound the sensitive lad.

"We shall reach Kooch's ranch by noon, and we are to rest there until it is cool again," he replied, flushing a little under her solicitous glance.

"Well, keep an eye on Shady!" said Blue Bonnet, waving him good-bye as she went to do her practising.

Fifteen minutes later each member of the ranch party was busily engaged in doing "just as she liked." Mrs. Clyde, deep in a book, sat under the fragrant magnolia; Kitty reclined on a Navajo blanket near her, lazily watching the gay-plumaged birds that made the tree a rendezvous. From the open windows of the living-room came a conscientious rendering of a "Czerny" exercise, enlivened now and then by a bar or two of a rollicking dance, with which Blue Bonnet sugar-coated her pill. In the kitchen Debby and Amanda were deep in the mysteries of "pinoche" under the tutelage of Lisa and Gertrudis; while Sarah, safe inside her own little sanctum, sat and drew threads rapturously, and later, coached by the delighted Benita, wove them into endless spider-webs.

CHAPTER V

THE SWIMMING HOLE

THEY sat up late that evening waiting for Alec to come with the mail. Mrs. Clyde and Blue Bonnet were somewhat uneasy, for they knew he had intended to be back in time for their late supper; and when ten o'clock came and no Alec or Shady appeared, they grew openly anxious.

Uncle Cliff refused to share their worry. "Shady's no tenderfoot," he scoffed, "and holding up the mail has gone out of fashion in these parts."

Blue Bonnet had no fear of hold-ups and did not care to express her suspicion that the ride had proved too much for Alec. She found reason to reproach herself: a forty-mile ride for a delicate boy like him was a foolish undertaking and she should have realized it. She had ridden that distance herself innumerable times; but she had practically been reared in the saddle and had lived all her life in this land of great distances. It was very different with Alec. The day of their picnic in Woodford came back to her, and again she saw the boy, worn out by a much shorter ride, lying white and unconscious before the fire in the hunter's cabin. She grew almost provoked with her grandmother for having insisted upon her practising instead of riding to Jonah as she had wished. If she had gone along, she at least would have known what to do for Alec in an emergency.

At eleven the moon came up, and rising out of the prairie simultaneously with the golden disk, came Shady, riding alone. A rapid fire of questions greeted him as he came up with the mail.

"Left the young fella at Kooch's," he explained briefly.

"What was the matter?" asked Blue Bonnet anxiously.

"Well, ye see—it was this way,—" Shady paused and then stood awkwardly shifting his sombrero from hand to hand. Blue Bonnet guessed instantly that Alec had sworn the cowboy to secrecy concerning the real reason for his non-appearance, and she refrained from further questioning. But her grandmother took alarm.

"Is he hurt—or ill?" Mrs. Clyde asked quickly.

For a moment Shady avoided her eyes, then resolutely squaring his shoulders he lied boldly: "No, Senora,—the mare went lame on him. He'll be over in the morning."

Mrs. Clyde drew a quick breath of relief; but Blue Bonnet was not so easily reassured. That Kooch had a dozen horses which Alec might have ridden if Strawberry was really disabled, was something her grandmother did not know; but the little Texan, used all her life to the easy give and take of ranch life, understood at once that Alec's real reason for staying at the Dutchman's was quite different from the one Shady had so glibly given. She knew better, however, than to press the cowboy, and let him go off to the cook-house without attempting to get at the truth.

"Grammy Kooch will take good care of him," said Uncle Joe; and with her fears thus set at rest, Mrs. Clyde proposed an adjournment to the house to read their letters.

The next morning Blue Bonnet was up before any one else in the house was stirring, and, dressing without arousing any of the other occupants of the nursery, she stole out of the house and made her way to the stable. Some of the Mexicans were already up, feeding the stock and doing the "chores," and one of them saddled Firefly. None of them wondered at Blue Bonnet's early appearance, for since her infancy she had ridden whenever the fancy took her, and now as she dashed out of the corral with Don and Solomon racing madly after her, the men grinned with satisfaction that the Senorita had returned to the ranch unchanged.

As she neared the Kooch ranch she saw a solitary horseman emerging from the gate. He was not looking towards her, and after a moment's scrutiny she began to whistle "All the Blue Bonnets." With a start of surprise Alec glanced up the road and at once galloped towards her.

"Is it really you?" he asked, hardly believing his eyes.

"Nae ither!" she laughed, turning Firefly and falling in with the strawberry mare—whose four legs, she noted, were as sound as ever.

"Well, you are an early bird."

"Lucky you're not a worm,—I'm hungry enough to eat one!" she said gaily. Under cover of the jest she stole a quick look at him. Yes, in spite of the sunburn he looked worn out and ill; he needed to rest and be taken care of. She refrained from asking how he felt and instead kept up a steady fire of nonsense, describing their dull day at the ranch without him.

If Alec had felt any resentment at her coming for him, it melted under her light treatment of the situation; and by the time they reached the little "rio" he was more like his usual, interested self.

"I think I'd like to follow up this cree—er—river, I mean," he remarked, looking up the winding, willow-grown course.

"Not before breakfast, thank you!"

"Well, I didn't mean right this minute, but sometime," he corrected.

"We will, surely. I want to introduce you to the lovely spots of the ranch, just as you showed me the charming places about Woodford. It will be different from following the brook as we used to do there, but I think you'll like it. There are picnic places along San Franciscito that can't be beat."

"San Frances*cheeto*?" he echoed; "where's that?"

"That's the name of this river," she replied loftily.

Alec threw back his head and laughed. "The name's bigger than the stream!" he declared.

"It has advantages over the brook, as you'll see. One of them is the swimming hole. Do you swim?"

Alec's eyes glistened. "I'm ready to learn."

"Well, get Shady to teach you. I'm going to make the girls learn. You boys and we girls will have the pool on alternate days,—won't it be fun?"

"The best ever. This is the first I've heard of it."

"I wanted some things for surprises," Blue Bonnet declared. "Isn't it odd your being here and seeing everything I used to talk about? It was a novelty then, but after this I won't have anything left to describe to you. What do you suppose we will talk about on our first jaunt by the brook next spring?"

Alec's face changed oddly. "Maybe there won't be any jaunt by the brook next spring—for me," he said, looking away from her startled eyes.

"Why, what do you mean?" she asked, and then wished she had not spoken, for she was suddenly afraid of his answer.

"I may not be,—you can't always tell," he stammered, looking as if he wanted to take it all back. "Let's not talk about it now, please," he begged, and Blue Bonnet gladly let the subject drop.

She rode on in silence the rest of the way, depressed and miserable. Alec's words were a revelation; she had not dreamed he felt so ill and doubtful of living. She had thought he would grow strong and well at the ranch, and already he was worse and spoke of his case as hopeless.

They were greeted with a loud outcry from the girls, who were perched on the top bar of the corral gate awaiting them. They had been somewhat startled upon arising to find Blue Bonnet gone, but Firefly's absence from his stall had explained her disappearance.

"Hurry up,—we're starving!" they cried; and Alec and Blue Bonnet, responding gaily, dismounted and hastened to the house with the rest, both glad to escape questions in the general hilarity and press of hunger.

"Grandmother," said Blue Bonnet later in the day; "I'm

worried about Alec." It was just after the siesta, and seeing her grandmother sitting alone in her chosen seat under the magnolia, she had gone out for a chat. They were seldom alone these days.

"He does look tired," Mrs. Clyde admitted; "but it is natural he should after that long ride."

"It isn't that." Blue Bonnet shook her head. "I'm afraid he's— got something."

"Got something?" her grandmother repeated in puzzled surprise.

"*Has* something, if you object to 'got.' Has something the matter with him, I mean,—serious, you know."

Then she repeated the conversation she had had with Alec that morning. Mrs. Clyde listened in silence, but her eyes were troubled when Blue Bonnet finished.

"It may not be so bad as Alec imagines," she said with a forced hopefulness. "He has been outgrowing his strength, and being overtired, too, makes him despondent."

In spite of her words, from that time on Mrs. Clyde was more observant of the boy, and the moment she saw the first signs of fatigue she would make some tactful suggestion for his benefit, relieving him of the necessity of saying he was tired, yet bringing about the possibility of rest. And often with her own hands she would concoct some nourishing dish, hardly so piquant as Gertrudis' red-hot creations, but rather more healthful for a growing boy. Neither she nor Blue Bonnet voiced their fears to the other girls nor to any of the men, but, with a silent understanding, ministered quietly to the frail boy's needs.

A few days later the girls crossed the meadow to the pool for their first lesson in swimming. It was an odd little bunch that sat on the bank dabbling their toes in the limpid water. The hastily improvised bathing-suits they wore were of every style and color, and they looked as gay as a flock of parrots in their bright-hued raiment. Blue Bonnet dove off the big boulder in the middle, to the great envy of the others, who only consented to get wet all over after much persuasion and the threat of a forcible ducking.

Sarah took the whole thing as seriously as she did most things. "Everybody should learn to swim," she announced authoritatively as she sat contemplating a plunge. "Some day we might have a chance to cross the ocean, and then we'd wish we knew how."

"Do you mean to swim across the ocean?" demanded Blue Bonnet wickedly.

"Of course not," replied Sarah, unruffled. "But in case of shipwreck, you know, it's well to be prepared. I believe it should be studied as a science,—get the stroke, then do it. It's like bicycle riding, they say: when you once learn how to keep your balance you never forget."

Blue Bonnet demonstrated the stroke again and again, while the other girls watched and imitated as they sat or sprawled on the grassy bank. Sarah bent her whole mind to the acquiring of the proper arm action; lay face-down and kicked scientifically; then, convinced of her preparation for the feat, boldly entered the water.

"Good for you, Sallikins!" cried Blue Bonnet. "The others must be afraid of getting their feet wet." Then she sang tauntingly:

"Mother, may I go out to swim?
Yes, my darling daughter,
Hang your clothes on a hickory limb—
But don't go near the water!"

Thus challenged, Kitty stepped shrinkingly into the cold water. "If Sarah will swim from me to you, I'll try it after her," she bargained. It was perhaps a distance of three yards from where she stood, waist-deep, to the big rock whereon Blue Bonnet was perched, laughing at them; but the Hellespont could hardly have loomed wider to the anxious eyes of Hero, than did this narrow channel now appear to the four novices.

"All right," agreed Sarah with dogged determination. She shut her eyes, screwed up her face, spread her arms, struck out with her feet and started. If a hippopotamus had suddenly slipped off the bank there could hardly have been a greater splash; Sarah kicked madly, puffing, panting, and churning the water into foam. All to no avail. Before she had gone a yard she sank like a paving-stone to the bottom of the pool. Blue Bonnet, convulsed with laughter, went down after her, but it took the combined efforts of herself and Kitty to bring the struggling Sarah to the surface. Sputtering and choking and much puzzled over the failure of her scientific method, Sarah retired to the bank to get her breath.

"Kitty's turn," she said inexorably as soon as she could speak.

Kitty found the bottom no less speedily, but scrambled up by herself and went at it again until she was able to progress almost two feet before going down to "call on the fishes," as Blue Bonnet said. It remained for Debby to cover herself with glory. Disdaining science and the instructions of the teacher, she took a lesson from Nature and struck out like a

C. E. Jacobs & Edyth Ellerbeck Read

puppy. Straight to Blue Bonnet she swam, struggled up on the big boulder beside her, gasping and breathless, but delighted at her own success.

"Bravo!" cried the girls, quite overcome with admiration.

Emboldened by her triumph the others tried again and again, and while not wildly successful were so far encouraged that they lost their first great fear of the water. And that, as every swimmer knows, is the first step towards victory.

"After you've all learned," said Blue Bonnet a little later, as they all sat on the veranda rail drying their hair, "we'll go over to the reservoir above Jonah some time and have a real swim. That is, if Grandmother's willing." She was glad she had remembered to add that last provision; it would have won an approving look from Aunt Lucinda.

"Then we'll have to have real suits," remarked Kitty, beginning then and there to plan a fetching costume for the occasion. "I'll write home for one right away."

When the plan was laid before Senora she made a brilliant suggestion. "Why not make your own suits? We may be able to find material in Jonah, and Benita and I will superintend."

Sarah beamed delightedly, but Blue Bonnet looked doubtful. "Will it be as hard as knitting a shawl?" she asked, ignoring the giggles her question provoked.

"Lots harder, you goose," said Kitty. "But if you begin it you'll probably have it finished for you by the same person who did the shawl."

"Then I don't mind!" Blue Bonnet agreed promptly. "We'll go to Jonah to-morrow—" adding before the words were fairly said, "—may we, Grandmother?"

"Perhaps," was all she said; but her eyes held more encouragement.

C. E. Jacobs & Edyth Ellerbeck Read

CHAPTER VI

AN ADVENTURE

"HAVE you decided, Grandmother," asked Blue Bonnet, "whether or not we can go to Jonah this morning?"

"I think you may as well go," said Mrs. Clyde. "If they have no suitable material at Jonah, we shall have to send away for it, and the sooner we know the better. And, besides, we need several things for the house."

Blue Bonnet smiled gratefully. Grandmother was so sweetly reasonable—most of the time. To her surprise Sarah was the only one of the girls who greeted the proposal with any enthusiasm. The others looked listless and heavy-eyed.

"I feel tired all over," said Debby.

"I can't move my arms without groaning," complained Amanda.

"I'm as stiff as a poker," added Kitty mournfully.

Sarah looked wise. "It's the swimming," she declared.

"Trying to swim," Blue Bonnet corrected her. "I'm not tired

or stiff."

"If trying to swim has made us feel this way, why doesn't Sarah make her little moan?" demanded Kitty.

Sarah looked still wiser. "I was so stiff before that I think swimming just limbered me up," she explained delightedly. Sarah could not help feeling a little very human satisfaction at the consciousness that she had borne her sufferings with far greater courage than the others now displayed.

"I couldn't ride a mile," groaned Kitty.

"Nor I!" declared both Debby and Amanda.

"Then, Senorita Blake, do we go by our lones?" asked Blue Bonnet.

"I'd love to," Sarah assented readily, beating down a nagging fear of Comanche's eyes.

"Then let's hurry and dress. We must start while it's cool."

"I think you will have to drive, dear," said her grandmother, looking up from the shopping list she was making. "Lisa says we must have laundry soap, and I don't see how you can bring a big box unless you take the buckboard."

Blue Bonnet's face fell. "Lisa's always wanting soap," she grumbled.

"I should love to drive," Sarah suggested wistfully.

Blue Bonnet hesitated; after all a hostess should consider a guest's preference, and Sarah was certainly a "good sort." "Very well," she assented, smothering a sigh.

"Have you all decided what color you want your bathing-suits?" asked the Senora.

"Let's have them all alike," suggested Sarah.

"Red!" exclaimed Blue Bonnet.

"No, thank you," returned Kitty. "Pray consider the feelings of my hair! I'm willing to have any color so long as—"

"—so long as it's green!" Blue Bonnet finished for her, recollecting former debates of this sort.

"Green is lovely for swimming, anyway," Kitty contended. "It's so mermaidy, you know."

"And so becoming to red—er—auburn hair," put in Blue Bonnet. "Having blue eyes myself, I'm not partial to green."

"Oh, if you're going to insist on harmony of colors I think we had better stick to black and blue—I'm one big bruise." Kitty illustrated her remark with a groan.

"Yes, I've seen blue trimmed with black and it was very pretty," said Sarah, quite missing Kitty's point.

"Here, Grandmother, please make a list. Now, everybody, decide. Red for me. Debby, what shall yours be?"

"Red with white braid, please," replied Debby after a moment's thought.

"Blue with white ditto," was Amanda's choice.

"Green," came from Kitty.

"Black and blue,"—this from the consistent Sarah.

"I think you will have to change the name of your club from the 'We are Sevens' to 'The Rainbow Quintet,'" said the Senora, laughing as she wrote down the variegated list.

After all it was a delightful drive to Jonah. The two fleet horses drew the light buckboard over the smooth road with a motion that Sarah found far preferable to the cat-like leaps of Comanche; and Blue Bonnet was so proud of being trusted to drive a team that she was quite reconciled to the arrangement.

"Denham would have fainted if I had even suggested driving Grandmother's carriage horses," she told Sarah, with a scornful sniff for those fat Woodford beasts.

"You drive beautifully," was Sarah's comforting rejoinder.

To their great satisfaction they found just what they wanted in Jonah. Alpaca was to be had in almost every shade, and wide white braid that made an excellent trimming. And to Blue Bonnet's delight she found a bright red sash that would add the finishing touch of elegance to her suit. Their shopping done and the buckboard well-heaped with their varied purchases, the two girls drove back as far as Kooch's ranch, where, according to an immemorial custom, they lunched and rested until the cool of the afternoon. On the return trip they met with an adventure.

The road ran for a short distance beside the little river with the big name—San Franciscito—which had so amused Alec. It was there that Sarah did something unprecedented. For several miles she had been envying Blue Bonnet her easy manner of handling the reins and the light touch that sent the mustangs right or left as she willed. It was a beautiful accomplishment.

"Blue Bonnet," she asked suddenly, "may I drive for a little while?"

Blue Bonnet looked up in speechless surprise; Sarah was certainly "coming on." "Surely you may," she said cordially, straightway handing over the reins. "Hold them firmly—these colts are apt to run under a loose rein."

Sarah felt a curious sense of power as she grasped the leather in her unpracticed hands. Conscientious to a degree, she did as she was bid and held the mustangs firmly. In her anxiety to do the thing properly, she overdid it, and the next moment the horses were tossing their heads angrily and backing with all their might. The bank of the stream just here was very high and steep, though just beyond was a ford where the road branched. The light buckboard offered no resistance to the spirited mustangs, and, in a second, before Blue Bonnet could grasp the reins, one hind wheel had slipped an inch or two over the ledge. For a second or two the girls were in grave danger. Blue Bonnet felt a swift overpowering fear; the half-broken colts were as apt to plunge backward as to advance if they felt the whip, and that meant a plunge down the steep bank. She looked about her helplessly. Sarah, with a faint shriek, shut her eyes and prepared for the catastrophe.

At that moment a horseman came suddenly up the bank at the ford, emerging as if from out the earth. At a glance he took in the situation, was off his horse, caught the near colt by the bit and brought both frightened animals to a standstill with the wheel a safe margin from the bank. Then without waiting to hear the faintly murmured thanks of the terrified girls, their rescuer turned at once to his own horse, which had seized the moment to make a break for freedom. The boy—for he was hardly more—had thrown the lines over the animal's head and now, with another of his incredibly swift movements, he caught them and in a second more had jerked the horse about. Then in a flash he was once more in the saddle. Blue Bonnet had just managed to catch her breath,— when it was taken away again. For before the boy had put his right foot in the stirrup, he was out of the saddle once more, lying all of a heap in the grass, while his horse with a wicked kick-up of his heels, vanished around a turn in the road.

Not daring to trust the reins out of her hands a second time, Blue Bonnet almost pushed Sarah from her seat. Fearfully the girl approached and bent over the fallen hero; to her relief she saw that his eyes were open. He blinked queerly for a moment, then gave a gaspy little laugh.

"I'm all right. Don't worry. It's knocked the breath out of me—that's all," he managed to say at last; and then, after another pause, he scrambled up to a sitting posture.

"I'm so sorry," said Sarah, finding her voice. "I hope you're not seriously hurt."

"I'm—quite whole!" he assured her, and stopped with a wince of pain. "It's my wrist, I reckon—broken or sprained." He examined the injured member closely and after a vain attempt to lift it said briefly: "Broken. Isn't that the limit?"

"Oh, dear," exclaimed Sarah, all sympathy. "What shall we do?" She approached Blue Bonnet with a very serious face. "We shall have to get a doctor to set his arm right away," she said in a low tone. "You know the bones go crooked if they're not set soon."

"If he can get up into the buckboard we can take him to the doctor, that'll be quicker," replied Blue Bonnet.

Sarah went back to the boy. He still sat, rather dazed and white, looking disgustedly at his injured arm. "Say," she began hesitatingly; she wished she knew his name—"say" was so plebeian; "—are you too badly hurt to get into the buckboard?"

"No, indeed," he replied cheerfully. "Be—with you—in a minute. But sorry—to trouble you."

"It's no trouble," said Sarah. "We're terribly sorry about your arm."

"Nothing much,—only a bother," he maintained stoutly, setting his teeth as he said it and scrambling to his feet. Then he swayed and would have fallen if Sarah had not caught him. He clung to her for a moment, fighting the dizziness with all the pride of his seventeen years, then giving in sheepishly, let her lead him to the buckboard. Once there he leaned weakly against the wheel, while the two girls, anxious and frightened, yet too considerate of his feelings to show their concern, watched him in speechless sympathy. At last he straightened up and gave a short, embarrassed laugh.

"Reckon I've got a funny-bone in my head," he said impatiently. Then steadying himself with his right hand he climbed slowly into the back seat of the buckboard.

"We'd better go to Jonah at once, don't you think—for the doctor?" Blue Bonnet asked him.

"Is it far?" he asked. Blue Bonnet looked her surprise and he added: "I don't know these parts. I'm camping up at the Big Spring and was just riding down this way looking for a place they call Kooch's."

"Why, we've just come from there," exclaimed Blue Bonnet.

"Then it is near?" he asked. "I'd begun to think I must have taken the wrong road."

"Just a mile or two back," explained Blue Bonnet.

"Then if you will kindly take me there, I'll not trouble you any further," the youth said eagerly.

"But you must have your arm set right away," protested Sarah.

"Well, if the man I was looking for is at Kooch's, maybe he can set it," he replied, adding, "He's a 'medic' from Chicago—a friend of a cousin of mine. Left college on account of lung trouble, and I heard he was camping on Kooch's ground somewhere."

"Maybe it was his tent we saw back there a ways," said Sarah. "That's quite near."

Blue Bonnet turned the horses and driving very slowly, so as not to hurt the boy's injured arm, went back over the road they had just traversed. It was not long before they came in sight of the tent she and Sarah had noticed; a rather high fence prevented her approaching it very closely, and she stopped just opposite the camp.

"I reckon you'll have to go and see if the man's there, Sarah," said Blue Bonnet.

Sarah looked fearfully at the high fence. "I just know I can't get over."

Blue Bonnet gave her a withering glance. "You— Woodfordite!" was the worst epithet she dared trust herself to before a stranger. "Then you'll have to hold the horses. There's no river to spill into here—and you don't have to pull them over backwards."

"There's no need, really," the young fellow interrupted. "I can bring Abbott if he's here." He raised his right hand, put the tips of two fingers to his lips and blew. The shrillest, most penetrating whistle the girls had ever heard pierced the air, causing the colts to lunge forward in a way that might have precipitated another catastrophe, had not Blue Bonnet's little steel wrist brought them up sharply.

At the summons a tall lanky figure appeared from within the tent and stood peering under his hand at the occupants of the buckboard. The youth whistled again, this time only with his lips,—a bird-like call. "That's his frat whistle. Ought to bring him."

And bring him it did. The lanky figure deserted the tent and with an eager stride crossed the meadow and came up to the fence. After one scrutinizing glance at the girls his eye fell on the boy and he grinned broadly.

"Hullo, Knight!—is it really you? Glad to see you, old chap!"

"Hello, Doc. How am I going to get over this hospitable fence of yours?" returned the boy, with an abruptness born of an aching wrist. "My nag threw me and I've broken my left arm. Know anybody that can set it?" He winked impudently at the fledgling doctor.

The latter beamed with professional delight. "Just my line, dear boy. I wish it had been your leg, now,—I do those beautifully!"

"Or my neck—I don't doubt it. But this is quite enough, thank you," retorted the boy. He was white with pain and yet could joke!—it was the sort of pluck Blue Bonnet admired.

"If your cousin will drive down to the gate,—" the young man suggested.

The boy looked a trifle embarrassed. "This isn't my cousin," he replied. "These gir—er—young ladies picked me up after my spill and—"

"I'm Elizabeth Ashe," Blue Bonnet supplied, coloring slightly.

"Of the Blue Bonnet ranch?" asked the medico, and at her affirmative nod he added, "I've met Mr. Ashe."

"This is Doctor Abbott," said the boy, striving to make the introduction easily, though one could see that such social amenities were not a matter of habit with him.

"I can't claim that title yet," the "doctor" protested. "My friends bestowed it when I was a freshman. I hope to earn it yet. Now, Knight,—about that arm. If Miss Ashe will drive on—there's a gate a hundred yards down the road. It isn't big enough to drive through, but I'll meet you there. I've some bandages in my tent. Be with you in a minute."

He appeared at the little gate bearing a most professional looking leather case and various packages that emitted queer odors. His enjoyment of the operation in store was plain.

"Hadn't I better go over to the tent with you?" asked the patient. To have an arm set with two strange girls looking on was evidently not to his taste.

"Too far for you to walk if you feel as shaky as you look," said Doctor Abbott, his keen eyes taking in young Knight's pale face and twitching lips. "And I may need assistance." He sprang lightly into the seat beside the patient and made a rapid examination. The girls resolutely kept their eyes away, but they could hear the boy's quick breathing. He made no other sound.

"A sprain, my boy," was the verdict which the girls heard with vast relief.

"Only a sprain?" asked Knight in an injured tone. "Then what makes it hurt so like the mischief?"

"A sprain hurts worse than a fracture, sometimes, but it is less serious and will heal quicker," said the doctor. "I've just the right thing here and will fix you up in no time."

The next five minutes were bad ones for the sufferer; Sarah and Blue Bonnet knew it, though they still stared off over the meadow and tried to chat unconcernedly, while the hurried breathing of the boy continued.

"There you are!" The girls turned to see the young man viewing his work and the neat bandage with approval, while Knight, with his lips still trembling, looked up at him with forced cheerfulness. "You'll have to keep it still for a few days,—wish we had some sort of a sling." Abbott knit his brow.

Knight touched the bandanna about his neck. "How about this?"

Abbott tried it but found it too short. Blue Bonnet had one of her sudden inspirations. Diving down underneath the seat she fished up one of the many packages. Under the interested eyes of the others she opened it and then held up something bright and silky.

"Your red sash!" gasped Sarah.

"Will it do?" Blue Bonnet asked the doctor anxiously.

"Just the thing!" he exclaimed; and in a minute had slung his patient's arm in the scarlet folds of the sash.

"I say," Knight protested, "I hate like everything to take this from you, Miss Ashe."

Blue Bonnet gave him a bright smile. "I'm very glad to have it prove so useful. Sarah called me frivolous when I bought it."

The boy looked uncomfortable but was forced to submit, vowing inwardly that he would buy her the "fanciest article in the sash line" that Chicago could boast, to make up for the loss of her finery.

"Now, my friend," said the young surgeon, as he gathered up his instrument case in a professional manner, "I must see that wrist in the morning. Where are you staying?"

The youth colored; it was evident that he had expected an invitation to stay with his friend. Blue Bonnet spoke up at once: "You must come with us to the ranch. Uncle would never forgive me if I let you stay anywhere else."

"Sorry I can't ask you to stay with me," Abbott said, observing the boy's confusion. "But I've only a cot built for one, you know. You'll be a heap more comfortable at the Blue Bonnet ranch than in my quarters. I'll ride over in the morning and take a look at you."

With the matter thus taken out of his hands, Knight had to submit. "It's mighty good of you," he said to Blue Bonnet.

"Not at all," she returned heartily. "I'd have to do a great deal to get even!"

"That wasn't anything," he protested. Then, turning to the doctor, he remarked with a return of his usual humor: "So long, Doc—hope you haven't injured me for life. Bring over your bill in the morning!"

CHAPTER VII

A FALLING OUT

IT was quite late when they reached the ranch, and an anxious crowd was awaiting them on the veranda. Blue Bonnet wished there were rather fewer people there; it was tiresome to make explanations before such an audience. Besides, she did not know the visitor's name,—introductions had been of a rather sketchy sort that day. Suddenly she made up her mind: she would explain nothing just then, and trust to her grandmother's ready tact to understand her reasons.

"This is—" Blue Bonnet looked at the youth inquiringly.

"—Knight Judson," he supplied.

"—and he's met with an accident and will stay here till his arm is better," she said rather breathlessly to her uncle.

"Very glad to have you, I'm sure," said Uncle Cliff with ready, outstretched hand.

Knight Judson took the proffered hand with an air of relief. "You're very kind, sir," he stammered.

"Not at all," Mr. Ashe protested cordially. "Come right in to supper."

They all went in without further ceremony to the delayed supper which Juanita stood waiting to serve; and the meal progressed in the usual gay fashion that prevailed at the ranch. Knight Judson was placed between Alec and Uncle Cliff, and in that congenial company the youth lost his shyness and was soon chatting away like an old friend. The awkwardness of eating with one hand gave him occasional bad moments, but little services, rendered unobserved by his attentive neighbors, tided over even these trying times.

The girls stole occasional glances down to that end of the table, which were promptly frowned upon by Blue Bonnet and Sarah. On the whole, they acted rather well considering the strain on their curiosity; it was not every day that a good-looking young chap, wearing a bright red sash for a sling, appeared at the ranch.

It was not until after supper, when Alec had taken the visitor to his room, that the others heard the whole story of the day's adventure. Sarah and Blue Bonnet told it almost together, a rather incoherent but wholly thrilling tale, while the rest of the girls hung breathlessly on the recital. Mrs. Clyde look worried when Sarah dwelt on the peril that had threatened the two of them; Blue Bonnet wished Sarah had not found it necessary to enlarge on that part of it. She, herself, preferred to describe young Judson's skill and quickness, his wonderful daring, and heroism under pain.

"Judson, Judson," repeated Sarah, wrinkling up her brow. "Where have I heard that name before?"

Blue Bonnet thought deeply for a moment. "I know," she cried; "don't you remember Carita, Carita Judson,—my missionary girl!"

"I wonder if they're related!" exclaimed Sarah. "She lives in Texas, you know."

"We must ask him in the morning," said Blue Bonnet.

Early the next day Mr. Ashe despatched one of the Mexicans with a letter from Knight Judson to his uncle at the Big Spring.

"Tell him not to expect you until he sees you," Mr. Ashe admonished the youth. "You must stay until that wrist is perfectly well."

"You're very good, sir," replied Knight warmly. He was not at all averse to spending any length of time in this pleasant place; he and Alec had fraternized at once, and he welcomed the chance to know the bright Eastern boy better; as for the girls, there were too many of them, he thought.

At breakfast Blue Bonnet opened fire on him.

"Carita!" he exclaimed. "Am I any relation to her? Well, I guess yes—she's my cousin! Do you know her?"

"I don't exactly know her," Blue Bonnet confessed, "—but we have—corresponded." She stopped abruptly; it was impossible to tell Knight about the missionary box; he might feel sensitive about it. Happily Sarah came to the rescue.

"Father knows the Reverend Mr. Judson," she remarked. "Is he your uncle?"

"Yes,—and Carita's father," he explained. "You see, Uncle Bayard has charge of a summer camp for boys up at the Big

Spring; he has had it for several years,—we have wonderful times there. A few days ago I had a letter from my cousin George in Chicago asking me to look up his friend Abbott, who had been ordered to Texas for his health. Abbott was at the Spring with us last summer, but it didn't agree with him, so he came to Kooch's. I was on my way there when—"

"When!" exclaimed Kitty dramatically. "We've heard what happened. We ought to have known better than to let a tenderfoot like Blue Bonnet go off with no protector but Sarah."

"It wasn't Blue Bonnet's fault," protested Sarah indignantly. "I was driving."

"And I suppose you drive as scientifically as you swim?" mocked Kitty.

Knight looked up with twinkling eyes; evidently the We are Sevens were not all of Sarah's type. Blue Bonnet he had already put in a class by herself.

"Please tell us some more about the boys' camp," begged Blue Bonnet, "I've heard about the Big Spring, and Uncle has promised to take me there. But, somehow, he never seems to get time. Is it a camp just for boys?—it sounds so interesting."

"It's one of Uncle's fads," Knight returned, showing by his tone that he was rather proud of "Uncle's fad." "He's tremendously interested in boys and has started a sort of 'get together' movement for fellows who live on big ranches and farms and don't get a chance to see much of other young people—"

"Like me!" Blue Bonnet nodded.

"They club in on expenses, share the work, and, incidentally, have more fun than some of them ever had before," he continued. "Uncle isn't at all strong—that's why he came back from his mission—but he works hard all the time, always doing good—" he stopped abruptly. "I didn't mean to brag, but when I get started on Uncle Bayard, I never know when to stop."

"And Carita—does she go camping, too?" asked Blue Bonnet.

"Aunt Cynthy often brings the whole family for over Sunday," he replied. Then a thought seemed to strike him. "Why don't you all come up and camp—it isn't a hard trip?"

Blue Bonnet clapped her hands. "Oh, I think it would be perfectly lovely. Grandmother, may we?" she asked.

Mrs. Clyde looked up with her sympathetic smile. "It sounds attractive. Perhaps we can arrange it."

Without seeming to do so Grandmother had heard every word of the conversation, and her heart had warmed to the boy who spoke so glowingly of his uncle's work. Knight Judson was a manly young fellow, she concluded, the right sort to be among girls; the best of companions for the frail, bookish Eastern lad.

Alec himself was charmed with Knight. There was something fascinating about a boy who had spent most of his life in the open, and without much aid from books had yet thought more deeply than most youths of his age. He was tall and strong, all bone and muscle, with something about him that was suggestive of a restless colt; but a thoroughbred, every inch of him.

After breakfast the two boys set out to hunt for Knight's horse, as nothing had been seen or heard of that frisky pony since he had vanished so unceremoniously the evening before. Alec carried a lariat, for learning to lasso had become the absorbing passion of his life, and young Judson, in spite of the hampering folds of the sling about his left arm, could give lessons in that art to any boy of his age in Texas.

Blue Bonnet and Mrs. Clyde looked after the youthful pair with interested eyes. It was plain that Knight had brought a new element into Alec's life, and these two good friends rejoiced, though they said nothing and only smiled with new understanding.

"I'm glad we nearly tipped over!" Blue Bonnet suddenly declared.

"Blue Bonnet!" exclaimed her grandmother in a pained tone.

"Well, I reckon I didn't mean that," confessed Blue Bonnet after a moment's reflection. "But I'm glad we've met Knight Judson. Alec has had too many girls around him here. He needs a spell of roughing it," and then, as she saw an odd look on her grandmother's face, she asked quickly: "Isn't 'roughing it' in good society?"

Mrs. Clyde laughed. "I believe it moves in the best circles— here."

"That's good, for there isn't a Massachusetts word that could possibly take its place."

"The dining-table is cleared, Benita says," Sarah announced from the doorway, "and we can begin our sewing lesson."

They all repaired to the house, and a few minutes later the

big dining-room was the scene of great activity; the table strewn with the bright-hued pieces of material, Benita smoothing and pinning the patterns, the Senora superintending, and the girls cutting and snipping to their hearts' content. At the same time there went on an incessant chatter, chatter, to the cheerful accompaniment of the sewing-machine.

When Juanita entered to spread the cloth for their early dinner, the girls looked up in surprise.

"I never knew time fly so quickly before," said Debby.

"If I'd known this kind of sewing was so easy and so fascinating," Blue Bonnet declared, "I'd have taken it up before. It's much nicer than embroidery or mending. Just see how much I've done!" She proudly held up the bright red garment.

Sarah scanned it with perplexed eyes. "It looks rather queer to me," she said.

Kitty examined it, too, then snatched the suit from Blue Bonnet's hands. "Look!" she bade the rest, "—there's no place to get into it. Blue Bonnet has sewn it up the back!"

There was a great outcry at this, which had the unexpected effect of making Blue Bonnet angry.

"There's nothing on earth gives Kitty Clark such pleasure as finding me out in a mistake," she declared with flashing eyes and cheeks that burned with mortification. Then she turned on Kitty,—"I'm sorry the ranch can't offer you any other enjoyment!" she said scathingly and then, snatching back her ridiculed work, flung herself out of the room.

Kitty's cheeks turned as red as her hair and she was just framing an angry reply to hurl after Blue Bonnet when she met Mrs. Clyde's eyes, full of a pained surprise. The girl checked the words on her lips at once, but a few hot tears came in spite of her efforts.

"I was only joking," she said with a catch in her voice.

"I'm afraid it was my fault," said Sarah. "I shouldn't have called attention to her mistake. I'll go and apologize."

Kitty turned to Mrs. Clyde. "I apologize to *you*, Senora," she said, adding proudly, "but I've nothing to apologize for to Blue Bonnet. Half the fun of being a We are Seven is being able to say just what we want to. If everybody is suddenly going to be thin-skinned, I'll have to go about muzzled."

"Blue Bonnet was hasty," said Mrs. Clyde, "and I'm sure she'll be ready to apologize as soon as she has thought it over."

The sewing lesson for that day ended in a gloomy silence. At dinner the two "magpies," as Uncle Joe had nicknamed them, were mute. This unheard of state of affairs would have aroused comment at any other time, but just now their attention was diverted.

"Doctor" Abbott, who had ridden over to "take a look at Knight's wrist," had stayed to dinner—there being always room for one more at that elastic table—and his bright humorous talk had completely fascinated every one. After dinner the men went off for a smoke, and the girls retired for their siesta in an atmosphere as hazy as if they too had indulged in the fragrant weed.

They went to the swimming hole later in the day, but somehow the zest was all gone from the sport, with the two leading spirits distrait and moody, avoiding direct speech with each other, and preserving an attitude of injured pride. Blue Bonnet had made up her mind that Kitty owed her an apology, while Kitty obstinately refused even in her thoughts to acknowledge herself in the wrong.

"Blue Bonnet thinks she's the king-pin of the universe," she mused angrily. "The others can keep on spoiling her if they want to, but I'm not going to kowtow all the time. They ape her every action,—*I'll* show her that one of us has independence."

Keyed up by this formula, repeated mentally a great many times, Kitty began to indulge in heroics. Aching to excite some admiration for herself she did "stunts" in the water that would have terrified her the day before. Once she plunged her bright head under the water and kept it there until she was almost black in the face, in an effort to prove her "staying powers." It only frightened the other girls and went apparently unnoticed by Blue Bonnet for whose benefit the test had been made.

"I'll show her we're not all 'fraid-cats!" Kitty resolved passionately. "I believe," she announced to the girls, in a tone loud enough to reach Blue Bonnet, who was doing an overhand stroke in the quiet water of the opposite bank. "*I* believe the only way to learn to swim is to dive in head-first—then you just *have to*. Big boys always toss little fellows into the middle of the pool and make 'em scramble back—they always do it right off. Here goes!"

She poised only for a moment on the bank, not daring to give herself time to reconsider. Blue Bonnet shot a quick glance at her; she saw at once that Kitty had chosen too shallow a spot,—a dive at that point might be dangerous. At any other

C. E. Jacobs & Edyth Ellerbeck Read

time she would have shouted a hasty warning, but now she hesitated,—and in that second Kitty shot head-first into the water.

The girls gave a gasp, and kept their eyes on the spot where she had gone down, waiting to see the red locks reappear. But the water closed over Kitty,—and stayed closed.

"Blue Bonnet!" they shouted shrilly, "she hasn't come up!"

Blue Bonnet felt a queer tightening around her heart; she had heard of boys breaking their necks that way. With a few powerful strokes she reached the shallows and felt for Kitty. "Help me girls—quick!" she cried, "she's struck her head on the bottom." She had seized Kitty by this time and held the girl's head above the water, but the body hung limp and heavy in her arms. The girls sprang to help and among them they managed to lift the slight figure to the bank and lay it tenderly on the soft grass. Kitty's face was deathly white, and from a gash on the top of her head a trickling stream was dyeing her bright locks a deeper red.

Blue Bonnet's teeth were chattering. "Go for somebody!" she gasped, and then, as Debby started on the run, she called after her—"That young doctor—bring him!" Then she turned to Sarah: "Here, help me set her up—work her arms—so!"

Dripping as she fled like a frightened water-sprite, Debby burst upon the others as they sat under the magnolia and screamed tragically:

"Come quick—the doctor, everybody! Kitty dove and Blue Bonnet went down after her and she's drowned!"

Then breathless, exhausted, and with her bare feet cut and bleeding from her run over the rough meadow, she fell headlong at Mrs. Clyde's feet.

Uncle Cliff dropped his pipe and ran, followed by the two boys and Abbott, who paused only to catch up his medicine case from the veranda, and then sped like the wind after the others. Mrs. Clyde had turned ghastly white at Debby's cry and had sprung up to follow the men. But the sight of the little messenger lying in a pathetic heap by her chair, stopped her. Hastily summoning Benita she helped carry Debby into the house and put her to bed; and not until a faint tired moan told of returning consciousness, did she yield to her anxiety and hasten to the pool.

With her feet winged by fear she crossed the meadow, ran as she had not run for forty years, and burst upon the group on the bank with a wild cry—"My girl, my girl—where is she?"

At the sound Blue Bonnet sprang up, and running to her grandmother hugged her convulsively. "She isn't dead—only stunned," the girl sobbed in a glad relief.

Mrs. Clyde held her off for a second. "It wasn't you then?" she questioned as if afraid to trust her eyes.

"No, no!" cried Blue Bonnet.

"Thank God!" breathed her grandmother. Then she folded the girl, wet as she was, in her arms, and held her close as if she would never let her go. In that moment Blue Bonnet knew and was never to forget how much she was loved by her mother's mother.

A sound drew them to the group about Kitty.

"There now!" young Abbott was saying cheerfully. "She's all right. Now, Knight, get in some of your good work,—first aid to the injured as taught by the Reverend Bayard Judson. A stretcher is what we need."

Much pleased to be called upon, Knight set about his task, while Alec supplied the place of his disabled arm. Under his directions two stout saplings were cut and the small twigs trimmed from them. Then stripping off his coat he bade Alec thrust the two poles into its sleeve, one in each. Uncle Cliff's coat went on at the other end; both coats were buttoned underneath, and there before the eyes of the interested group, was a stretcher ready for the patient.

Kitty, still weak and dazed, but with the color beginning to return to her milk-white cheeks, was borne gently to the house by Uncle Cliff and the doctor, attended by a body-guard of Alec and Mrs. Clyde, and followed by the other dripping and subdued We are Sevens.

There was a rather bad quarter of an hour for Kitty while the doctor bathed and dressed her wound. After much debating and grave consideration in his most profound manner, young Abbott had decided that the cut was not deep or wide enough to warrant his sewing it up. Whereat there was great rejoicing in the household,—not, however, shared by the medical man. A bit of stitching would have given him practice and no end of professional enjoyment. However, Kitty felt that she had had quite her share of attention and was glad to be left alone in the nursery tucked in between cool sheets, to sleep off the ache in her broken head.

When she awoke it was dusk in the room. Beside her bed stood somebody, bearing a tray.

"Are you awake?" asked a sepulchral voice.

"Yes," she whispered faintly.

The tray was hastily placed on a stand, a second pillow slipped deftly under Kitty's head, and then before she had recognized her servitor a pair of soft lips were laid on hers and a penitent voice whispered: "I'm so sorry, Kitty,—and ashamed!"

"It wasn't your fault, Blue Bonnet," said Kitty, returning the kiss warmly. "Served me right for being such a peacock."

"Then all's serene on the Potomac?" Blue Bonnet questioned.

And with a reassuring, though somewhat shaky smile, Kitty returned:

"All's serene!"

CHAPTER VIII

CONSEQUENCES

BLUE BONNET came in from an early morning romp with Don and Solomon looking even more rosy and debonair than usual. It was surprising how much easier it was to rise early at the ranch than it had been at Woodford. She liked to steal quietly out of the nursery and go adventuring before breakfast; she felt then like Blue Bonnet the fourteen-year-old, full of the joy of life, untroubled by fears of any sort or desires for the great unknown. She and Don in those days had had many a ramble before the dew was off the grass. Hat-less and short-skirted she had climbed fences, brushed through mesquite and buffalo grass; hunted nests of chaparral-birds; sat on the top bar of the old pasture fence and watched the little calves gambolling; or, earlier in the spring, had gathered great armfuls of blue bonnets from over in the south meadow. Now when she found herself away from the house, skirting San Franciscito in an eager chase for a butterfly, she could have thought the past ten months all a dream,—except for a certain small brown dog tearing madly from one gopher-hole to another, while Don, in the veteran's scorn for the novice, refused to be enticed from his mistress' side.

"Where's Grandmother?" she asked as she entered the dining-room. Grandmother always sat at the head of the breakfast table, and her sweet "homey" face over the teacups, was the first thing Blue Bonnet looked for.

"Benita says the Senora is not well," replied Juanita.

The brightness all went out of the morning. Grandmother breakfasting in bed! It was unheard of. In her impetuous rush from the room Blue Bonnet almost collided with Benita. "Is Grandmother awake—can I go to her?" she asked, impatiently.

"It is better not. The Senora prefers to rest," said Benita.

"What's the matter with her, Benita? I never knew Grandmother to be ill before," Blue Bonnet asked miserably.

"It is the shock, I think. The Senora is not so young as she once was, Senorita."

Blue Bonnet turned away, sick at heart. In the nursery she found nothing to improve her spirits. Kitty lay languid and pale among her pillows, saying that her head ached and she didn't care for any breakfast. Debby, too, had kept her bed, declaring that she couldn't bear shoes on her poor lacerated feet. Amanda and Sarah only appeared as usual, and these two had their spirits dampened immediately by the sight of Blue Bonnet's gloomy countenance.

The three of them had the table to themselves, the men having breakfasted earlier than usual and Alec and Knight having hurried through the meal and ridden off, no one knew where. Blue Bonnet was not conversational; everything in her world seemed topsy-turvy, and she felt that she must have an hour of hard thinking to sort things out and put them in their places.

Amanda and Sarah, respecting Blue Bonnet's mood, were silent. During this period of unusual restraint, a resolution was forming in Amanda's mind, and at the conclusion of the meal she made an announcement that would have petrified the rest had it come at any other time.

"I'm going to study," she said.

Sarah looked her approval of this decision. "I'll help you,— let's do it in my room."

Relief on Blue Bonnet's part quite crowded out surprise. "Then you don't mind if I leave you to yourselves?" she asked.

"We wouldn't get much done if you didn't," Amanda replied with more frankness than tact.

Blue Bonnet had found solitude glorious in the half-hour before breakfast, but now it had lost its charm: joy in her heart had given place to hate. Not hatred of the old life, such as had driven her to pastures new; not hatred of Texas and "all it stood for"—as she had once passionately declared to Uncle Cliff. This time the object of her deep and bitter feeling was—herself. She had been rude to a guest in her own house. She had seen one of her best friends risk her life and had made no move to prevent it. She had been the cause of her grandmother's receiving a shock which, at her time of life, might prove very serious. And all this in spite of having lived for nearly a year with two such perfect gentlewomen as Aunt Lucinda and Grandmother Clyde. In spite of her boasted loyalty to the "We are Sevens." In spite of her promise to her aunt to care tenderly for her grandmother and bring her back safely to Woodford.

She had wandered aimlessly outdoors and now flung herself

face down on the Navajo under the big magnolia. "It's no use,—I reckon it's the same old thing. I'm not an Ashe clear through." With the thought came swift tears.

Her head lay against something hard and unyielding; and after her first grief had spent itself, she put up her hand to push away the object—but grasped it instead. It was a book; opening her tear-wet reddened eyes Blue Bonnet saw that it was a volume of her grandmother's favorite Thoreau. It lay just where Mrs. Clyde had dropped it the day before when she had sprung up at Debby's frightened cry.

She dried her eyes and sat up. Leaning against the low, wicker chair, that was her grandmother's chosen seat, she slowly turned the leaves of the well-worn volume, her thoughts more on the owner of the book than on its author. All at once her glance was caught and held by something that seemed an echo of the cry that kept welling up from her own unhappy heart. It was a prayer, only ten short lines, and she read them with growing wonder:

"Great God! I ask thee for no meaner pelf
Than that I may not disappoint myself;
That in my striving I may soar as high
As I can now discern with this clear eye.
That my weak hand may equal my firm faith,
And my life practise more than my tongue saith.
That my low conduct may not show,
Nor my relenting lines,
That I thy purpose did not know
Or over-rated thy designs."

How could any one, and that a grown man and a poet, have so exactly voiced the thoughts of a young girl on a far-off Texas ranch?

" . . . . I ask thee for no meaner pelf
Than that I may not disappoint myself."

That was just it—she had disappointed herself, grievously, bitterly. So absorbed was she that she did not hear a foot-fall, nor did she look up until Uncle Cliff exclaimed, "All alone, Honey? That doesn't often happen these days!" His cheerful voice expressed no regret for the absence of the others.

She looked up, and then quickly down again; but not soon enough for the traces of tears to escape his watchful eye.

"What's up, Blue Bonnet?" he asked anxiously. He was on the rug beside her now, and with a hand under her quivering chin tilted her face and scanned it closely.

She winked fast for a moment. "Uncle Cliff, do you find it terribly hard to be good?"

"Thundering hard, Honey." He thought whimsically that it was lucky no one else had heard that question. "So hard that my success at it hasn't been remarkable!"

"Oh, Uncle, it has!" she declared. "And it always seems so easy for you to 'live as you ride—straight and true.' I was so proud last winter when you said I'd proved I was an Ashe, clear through. But I reckon you spoke too soon. I've been showing what Alec calls 'a yellow streak.'"

"Don't you say that of my girl! I'll wager our best short-horn against a prairie-dog that if you've a yellow streak it's pure gold!" He caressed the brown head that nestled against his arm.

She wriggled away and faced him firmly. "You may as well know the worst, Uncle Cliff. It was my fault that Kitty was hurt yesterday. It's my fault Grandmother is ill and Debby's feet hurt. I was mean and thoughtless and selfish and—"

He put his hand over her mouth. "Look here, no Ashe is going to hear one of his race called all those ugly names. Remember whom you're talking to! Things always seem to come in bunches, Honey, but you have to dispose of them one at a time. Why, it's hardly a year since a girl about your size—a bit younger she was, but she had blue eyes just like yours,—was saying she reckoned she'd never make a Westerner, and she hated the ranch and was going to sell it as soon as she came of age—"

"Don't!" came in a smothered tone from Blue Bonnet. Her face was buried again. "Don't remind me how downright horrid I was."

"And six months later that same little girl—blue eyes same as yours—was telling me how she reckoned that three hundred years would never make an Easterner of her, and she loved the ranch and wanted to be a Texas Blue Bonnet as long as she lived!"

"And so I do, Uncle."

"Well, I'm just running over a few items in order to remind you that most troubles aren't half as black as your feelings paint them at the time. It's best not to worry over spilt milk till you see it's made a grease-spot. Ten to one the cat will lick it up,—and it's an ill wind that blows nobody good. There,—that figure of speech is as mixed as a plum-pudding, but it has a heap of sound philosophy!"

Blue Bonnet was smiling now. "I wish all the preachers would say the kind of things you do. Most of the sermons I've heard sound like that last piece of mine—'variations on one theme'—and the theme is Duty with a big D. Sarah was brought up on those. And they must be pretty successful, for Sarah is awfully good. Isn't she?"

"Just that—awfully good."

She looked up quickly, struck by something odd in his tone; but he was perfectly sober.

"She's the salt of the earth," he added, "and you—"

"And what am I?"

He smiled down at her. "Do you remember how the south pasture looks when the blue bonnets bloom in March,—how fresh and sweet, a sky turned upside down—? It's the glory of the ranch, Honey. And what they are to the ranch, you are to me. Please don't be trying to be something you can't be, Blue Bonnet!"

She laughed outright. "That sounds like the Duchess in 'Alice in Wonderland.' Don't you remember?"

"I confess I don't. You've been neglecting my education, young lady, since you began your own. What does the Duchess say?"

"'Be what you would seem to be'—or, if you want it put more simply—'Never imagine yourself not to be otherwise than what it might appear to others that what you were or might have been was not otherwise than what you had been would have appeared to them to be otherwise.'" The face she turned to him as she finished was cloudless, and he breathed a sigh of relief.

"That's quite plain," he said, "and I hope you'll take the

lesson to heart!"

She smiled as she rose. Glancing up he was surprised to see how tall she looked,—quite as tall, he thought, as her mother had been when she came a bride to the ranch. Well, she was almost sixteen,—the other Elizabeth was only eighteen.

"You've done me a lot of good, Uncle Cliff," she was saying. "I think my 'indigo fit,' as Alec calls the blues, has faded to a pale azure, and I can go to Grandmother. She will be wondering where I am."

"Next time I see a fit coming on, I shall quote the Duchess!" he warned her.

Blue Bonnet was delighted to find her grandmother awake and ready for a "heart to heart" talk. Snuggled cosily on the bed at her feet the penitent poured out all her discouragement of the morning, and received the balm, which like the milk in the magic pitcher, bubbled constantly in Grandmother's heart.

In Sarah's room the two students were diligently at work, Sarah in the role of preceptress, hearing Amanda's French verbs, or helping to discover the perplexing value of X in an algebraic equation. Only occasionally did the thoughts of either wander.

"This is the second time," remarked Amanda, "that Blue Bonnet and Kitty have had a tiff. The 'third time never fails,' you know."

"Do you really think that after the third falling-out they'd stay—"

"Out?—indeed I do think so," Amanda declared. "I've seen it

C. E. Jacobs & Edyth Ellerbeck Read

come true too many times to doubt it. There are always three fires—the last the worst; three spells of illness, three shipwrecks, three—everything!"

"It sounds rather—superstitious to me," observed Sarah, doubtfully. "I shouldn't like to believe it anyway, for it keeps you always looking out for the third time, and that is *so* uncomfortable."

"It's true as gospel," Amanda insisted.

From that time onward, in spite of her better judgment, Sarah lived in perpetual dread of Blue Bonnet's third falling-out with Kitty; and her attitude was continually that of the pacifier, pouring the oil of tactful words on troubled waters, or averting the wrath of either by a watchfulness that never relaxed. Just how much was due Sarah for the cordial spirit that prevailed for a long time following this between the two girls, neither realized; and Sarah asked no reward for her pains, save peace.

CHAPTER IX

TEXAS AND MASSACHUSETTS

AT supper-time all the invalids were up; Kitty appearing rather "interestingly pale," as Amanda remarked; Debby hobbling about in padded bedroom slippers; and Grand-mother Clyde looking somewhat older and grayer than usual, but calm and contained once more.

"Where are the boys?" asked the Senora, noting Alec's absence with some anxiety.

"They went off early this morning loaded for big game," said Uncle Joe with a twinkle in his eye.

"Do you mean they carried guns?" Mrs. Clyde spoke with a shade of worry in her tone; she had missed the twinkle.

"Shady had a shotgun, I believe, but the boys carried nothing deadlier than lariats. I believe young Trent takes one to bed with him. He's been practising on the snubbing-post in the corral for hours every day,—he's got so he catches it about once in so often, and he's tickled to death." Uncle Joe chuckled.

"Knight Judson can beat any of the Mexicans at lassoing,"

C. E. Jacobs & Edyth Ellerbeck Read

Blue Bonnet declared. "He must be a wonder when he has both hands free."

"He doesn't seem in any hurry to discard his sling, I notice," Uncle Joe remarked, winking at Blue Bonnet ostentatiously.

"His wrist isn't well yet," she insisted, ignoring the teasing glance.

"Here they come, now," exclaimed Kitty. "Alec looks as excited as if he'd killed a bear at the very least!"

"We've had a wonderful day," Alec declared, full of enthusiasm, when he and Knight had greeted every one and slipped into their places. Both boys were ravenous; Blue Bonnet and her grandmother exchanged a significant glance as Alec passed his plate for a second generous helping. He looked already a different boy from the pale student who had left Woodford only a few weeks before.

"Guess what we bagged to-day?" he asked.

"A bear!" Kitty said immediately.

"Quail!" Blue Bonnet guessed.

"Shady got some quail, but we didn't do any shooting," replied Alec.

"Maybe you and Knight lassoed some prairie-hens," suggested Uncle Joe, laughing at his own joke.

"Alec lassoed his first steer all right—made a neat job of it too," said Knight enthusiastically.

"Very amateurish work," Alec protested, pleased nevertheless at Knight's praise. "The steer thought I looked so harmless that he took a big chance—that's how I came to land him."

"But what did you 'bag?'" asked Blue Bonnet, going back to the original question. "Is it good to eat?"

Knight and Alec exchanged amused glances. "Never tasted them," both declared.

"Where is it?" Blue Bonnet persisted.

"'Tisn't 'it,'—but 'they'—and they're out in the barn," said Alec, delighting in the mystery.

Blue Bonnet was all impatience. "Oh, do hurry, everybody, and let's go see," she urged.

The rapidity with which Knight and Alec ate the rest of their supper should have given them indigestion, even if it did not. It was impossible to leave any of Gertrudis' raspberry tart; equally impossible to keep their hostess waiting when she was on tip-toe to be off; mastication therefore was the only thing they could neglect—and did.

Blue Bonnet had felt all the weight of her sixteen years a few hours earlier, but now she seemed to drop at least six of them, as she raced across the yard, impelled by a curiosity that Kitty would have died rather than display.

Don and Solomon were sniffing excitedly about one of the mangers, emitting an occasional shrill bark; Blue Bonnet went straight to it and peered down. It was too dark to make out anything, but she could hear a rustling in the hay, and a pathetic, low whine.

"It's something alive!" she cried, and was about to put an

C. E. Jacobs & Edyth Ellerbeck Read

exploring hand down to find the source of the whine, when she had a second thought. "Will it bite?"

"Too little," Knight assured her. He bent as he spoke and lifted two little furry bundles and laid them in Blue Bonnet's outstretched arms.

"Puppies!" she cried delightedly. She bore them to the light, the other girls crowding about for a view of the wriggling mites.

After her first good look at them, Sarah gave an exclamation of surprise. "Why, they're not dogs," she cried.

"Yes, they are," said Alec, "—coyote pups!"

"Oh, the dears!" cried Blue Bonnet ecstatically. "Where did you get them?"

"Shady shot the mother," Knight explained, and then wished he had not,—Blue Bonnet looked so grieved. "She killed a calf a few nights ago," he said in extenuation, "and Shady was 'laying for' her. She made for her hole after she was wounded and we followed,—that's how we came to find the pups. Lucky we did or they'd have had a hard time of it."

"Poor babies," said Blue Bonnet. "Let's go and show them to Grandmother and Debby—I reckon they never saw a real live coyote before. Here, Sarah, you carry one." She generously held out one of the bright-eyed babies, but to her surprise Sarah drew back. "Why, you can't be afraid, Sarah?"

"N-no," Sarah replied, edging away as she spoke. "But I don't like to touch—live animals."

"Well, I'd much rather touch live ones than dead things!"

exclaimed Blue Bonnet. "Here, Alec, you take the poor baby—Sarah doesn't know how to mother it!"

Grandmother and Debby were rather lukewarm in their praise, Blue Bonnet thought, when the coyotes were brought to them on the veranda. Grandmother did not look in the least delighted when the two sharp-nosed, long-haired puppies were dropped into her lap; and finally Blue Bonnet gathered them both in her arms, declaring that nobody knew how to appreciate real Texas babies except herself.

"I'm going to keep them always," she said. "And Don and Solomon will just have to be reconciled."

"Have you asked your uncle if he is willing for you to keep two such pets?" her grandmother asked.

Blue Bonnet looked over to Uncle Cliff and laughed. "Asked Uncle Cliff? Why, Grandmother, I brought him up and he knows better than to oppose me at this late day!"

Uncle Cliff smiled back at her whimsically. "I hope I'm a credit to your training! Two new pets is quite a modest demand. I've known her to have a dozen or two at a time. One summer she had twin lambs, a magpie, a lizard, bunnies—"

"Don't forget the snakes," Blue Bonnet interrupted.

"Blue Bonnet Ashe—you never made pets of snakes!" gasped Debby.

"Three of them; beauties, too," Blue Bonnet replied.

"Weren't you afraid of them?" Sarah asked wonderingly.

"These were perfectly harmless; nobody should be afraid of such pretty little things. But the magpie had fits over them, so they had to go," Blue Bonnet remarked regretfully.

"What became of the magpie?" asked Kitty.

"Poor Mag died of curiosity," said Mr. Ashe. "She sampled some cyanide of potassium I had put out for ants. We had a most impressive funeral. You must get Blue Bonnet to show you her grave."

"I will some day. We chose Mag's favorite spot—under a dewberry bush. Now what shall we call these cherubs?"

"You've just called them 'Texas babies,' why not call one 'Texas?'" Knight suggested.

"And the other 'Massachusetts,'" said Sarah.

Blue Bonnet looked at her in open admiration. "Your inspirations don't come often, Sarah," she remarked, "but they're as apt as not to be positively brilliant when they get here! Texas and Massachusetts the babies shall be. Poor Massachusetts' name is as long as his tail, but maybe he can bear up under it."

"Let's go show them to the youngsters," Alec suggested. "Pancho's twins are straining their eyes for a peep."

Blue Bonnet gave him one of the pups to carry and together they crossed the yard to the Mexican quarters. A moment later Blue Bonnet was sitting in the doorway of the little adobe hut, the coyotes in her lap, while all of Pancho's brood, not to mention Pancho and his fat Marta, were hanging about her in an eager, admiring circle. Every little "greaser" on the ranch adored the Senorita, and she was godmother to half the babies born on the place. Alec bade fair to be almost as popular as she, for he was always ready for a romp and had an unfailing supply of nuts in his capacious pockets. The visit now ended in a "rough-house," Alec with his ever-handy lariat lassoing the fleet-footed boys and pretending to take them prisoner, while they dodged and ran and kept up a shrill chorus of baby Spanish that delighted his soul.

Later he and Blue Bonnet walked to the stable and put the coyotes down for the night; choosing the unused manger again as being secure against the impertinent investigations of Don and Solomon, and deep enough to prevent the venturesome babies from falling out. It was almost dark as they strolled back towards the house, lingering and chatting and drinking in the beauty of the night. The lovely southern sky was studded with stars; the breeze laden with perfumes that only a Texas prairie knows; and the air full of melody,— the deep laughter of the cowboys lounging about the bunk-house, and the sweet tone of Shady's fiddle as he played to the crowd on the house-veranda.

Alec paused and drew a deep breath. "And you wanted to leave it!"

"I wonder at myself sometimes," she confessed. "But I'm not sorry. Think how much richer I am this summer than last, with Grandmother and all the girls,—not to mention present company!"

"Thank you!" Alec laughed and made his bow.

"You like it more because it is—different, than for any other reason. I reckon you have to know other places before you can properly appreciate your own," she went on thoughtfully.

"This doesn't seem to add to my appreciation of—Woodford," Alec rejoined quickly.

"That's because you haven't been here long enough. After a few years you'd begin to wonder how the elms look on Adams Avenue, and yearn for a glimpse of the Boston Common—just as I used to long for a sight of the prairie. But I'm glad you like it here—for it is a grand old place!"

"I wish Grandfather would rejoice because I like it," he remarked moodily. "He seems to be sorry that I didn't go abroad with Boyd. And Boyd's letters to him—which he always forwards—are full of ravings about automobiles and scenery and pictures. Pictures!" Alec pointed to the meadow ahead of them where a million fireflies flashed their tiny lanterns, "—I wish he could see this! And I wish—I wish I could make him understand the bigness of it all. And how tired I am of sitting still and letting other people *do* things. I want to live." The boy's voice trembled as he ended.

Again Blue Bonnet had a sudden sinking of the heart—could Alec mean—? She opened her lips to speak, but he went on gloomily:

"Grandfather doesn't seem able to understand. He has never been willing to admit that I am a weakling, and refuses to see that my days are numbered in Woodford. I've been trying to get up courage enough to write him about myself, but I can't do it—yet." And then, as if fearing he had said too much, he added: "But don't say anything to the others, please. It's too soon—I may feel different by the end of the summer. Let it be a secret between us two—three rather, for I've already told Knight." Then, before Blue Bonnet could gather herself together for a reply, he had started on a new tack. "I tell you, Blue Bonnet, there's a fellow that dwarfs every other chap I ever knew!" His tone was now as eager and enthusiastic as it had been doleful.

Blue Bonnet was puzzled, but deciding that Alec needed to have his mind turned from introspective subjects, she took him up at once. "I agree with you. He's a giant for his age."

"I don't mean his size," returned Alec. "He's so big— mentally, you know. And he's so alive, so—"

"Up and coming?" interpolated Blue Bonnet. "That's pure Texan, I believe."

"It describes him exactly."

"What I can't understand is how such an expert horseman came to be thrown," Blue Bonnet remarked wonderingly.

"I suppose he was startled at seeing a blue bonnet out of season!" laughed Alec. "I'm so glad something happened to bring him my way. It seems to give me a new lease on life just to be with him."

"Uncle Cliff says he is 'greased lightning' with a lariat," said Blue Bonnet.

"I should say he is. I could find it in my heart to envy him that accomplishment, even if he hadn't any others."

"Uncle Joe says you are getting quite expert yourself," she threw out comfortingly.

"Oh, yes, I can lasso a snubbing-post that can't get out of the way!" he retorted. He still clung to his lariat and now swung it in his hand rather impatiently.

"Try your skill now. There's one of the girls waiting for us—

C. E. Jacobs & Edyth Ellerbeck Read

lasso her and see how she acts!" Blue Bonnet urged mischievously.

"Where?"

"There—just by the magnolia," she whispered.

It was almost dark, but Alec could manage to make out a dark figure standing half within the shadow of the big tree. He crept silently a few steps nearer and paused, whirling the loop around his head. The hair rope spread into a circle, hissed and flickered for a moment in the air, then dropped straight over the victim. It was a good throw. Alec gave a twitch—not too hard—to the lariat, and the thing was done. Blue Bonnet clapped her hands and started forward with Alec to see which one of the girls he had caught. Both suddenly stopped in dismay. There was a struggle, a shrill scream, and a very angry Spanish oath.

And as the two of them hastened up full of surprise and apologies, they saw—Juanita and Miguel both caught in the one noose.

Stifling their laughter, Alec and Blue Bonnet released the embarrassed pair of sweethearts, and then the boy made a handsome apology. Juanita hung her head and was silent, but Miguel, after the first blazing up of his anger, cooled down and accepted the explanation in good part.

Still weak with suppressed laughter, the two miscreants hurried on, waiting to be out of ear-shot before giving way to their wild mirth. As they drew near to the veranda they heard the crowd there singing to the accompaniment of Shady's violin.

"Nita, Jua-a-an-ita, ask thy soul if we must part!"

came tremulously from Uncle Joe and the We are Sevens.

It was too much. Blue Bonnet collapsed in a heap on the grass.

"Oh, Alec!" she gasped. "Miguel ought to have been singing that,—only he ought to have said—'Jua-a-an-ita, bless my soul if we can part!'"

CHAPTER X

ENTER CARITA

TWO days later Knight appeared at the table minus his sling, and announced that this must be his last day at the ranch. There were expressions of regret from everybody, and from Blue Bonnet vigorous objections. The boy quite glowed under the tribute.

"I simply must go," he protested firmly. "Though it's a big temptation to stay, I tell you. But it isn't fair to Uncle Bayard for me to be away any longer. Those twelve boys keep things moving for him. I hope you will be able to come up for one of our Sundays," he said to Mrs. Clyde.

"Grandmother has missed her church more than anything else," Blue Bonnet remarked. "It's been pretty warm to drive to Jonah, and none of the Padres has visited the ranch since we came."

"We have an outdoor service in a beautiful grove of trees," Knight explained, "and that setting and the boys' voices in the open air and all—well, it has spoiled me for stuffy meeting-houses. Can't you all come up and stay over next Sunday?" His glance and the eyes of all the We are Sevens were fastened anxiously on Mrs. Clyde's face.

She thought for a moment. "It seems a stupendous under-taking,—for so many of us," she said at length. Camping out in Texas was full of unknown and rather dreadful possibilities, she secretly opined.

"We'll take all the responsibility, Grandmother," Blue Bonnet assured her gravely.

Mrs. Clyde did not meet her granddaughter's eye; that young lady's method of taking responsibility was not such as to inspire one with unlimited confidence.

"I can send Miguel ahead with one of the cook-wagons," Uncle Cliff suggested. "You can have Pancho, too, if you like,—he cooked on the round-up this spring and didn't kill anybody. Lisa's too fat and Gertrudis too old for that ride."

"And we want Lupe for wrangler," said Blue Bonnet. "A wrangler looks after the horses, Sarah *mia*," she explained, anticipating the question.

"If we go," said Senora, "let us go as simply as possible. Surely we don't need such an army of men."

"But, Grandmother," Blue Bonnet protested, "there has to be a cook, and somebody to pitch tents, and one to look after the horses and—"

"I don't see the necessity. You miss half the pleasure of camping out if you have everything done for you. When I was a girl we used to camp out in the Maine woods, and we girls took turns cooking and washing dishes, while the boys gathered wood for the fires, caught fish and looked after the horses. To take a crowd of servants along would rob the life of all its simplicity."

Blue Bonnet looked rather blank. Cooking and washing dishes did not seem altogether simple to her.

"I can make caramel cake," announced Kitty.

"That's lovely—especially for breakfast," said Blue Bonnet.

"I don't like sweet things for breakfast," said Sarah.

"Beans and bacon are as good camp fare as one needs," said Knight. "It is pretty cool in the mornings and evenings, and one gets hungry enough to eat the dishes."

"We'll agree to anything if Grandmother will only go," said Blue Bonnet eagerly.

Grandmother, however, withheld her decision until she had held a serious conversation alone with Uncle Cliff.

"Don't you think you are encouraging Blue Bonnet in habits of extravagance?" she asked, smiling inwardly at the likeness of her question to some of Lucinda's.

Uncle Cliff pondered for a moment. "That depends on what you call 'extravagance.' According to my definition it means spending more than you can afford."

"Blue Bonnet is certainly spending a great deal this summer. It must cost something to keep up a big place like this, so many servants besides all the guests."

"Mexicans don't draw down princely salaries, you know," he argued. "And we're not used to counting noses at table. Besides, Blue Bonnet has enough to do just about as she likes with. Miss Clyde and I had some talk about it last winter—when she put the poor child on an allowance. Three dollars!" Mr. Ashe made a comical grimace. "Why, Mrs. Clyde, I've been putting by Blue Bonnet's profits every year for nearly sixteen years, and they've been pretty tidy sums, too. Besides, she's going to have every penny of mine, some day. And now she's old enough to enjoy spending, I don't quite see the use of making her skimp." He looked very much in earnest and ready to "have it out" then and there.

"But the possessors of wealth should be taught the value of money, just the same, don't you think so?" Mrs. Clyde urged.

"Surely!" he agreed. "And Blue Bonnet has a very fair idea of its value, I think. She gives more people a good time on it than any one I know. You never knew her to stay awake nights worrying over something for herself, now did you?"

"Blue Bonnet is not given to worrying over anything. Not that I wish her to. She is dear and warm-hearted and generous like her mother, but a little heedless,—Lucinda thinks. She needs to be taught that wealth entails responsibility."

"Lucinda!" was Mr. Ashe's mental ejaculation. He might have known the source of Mrs. Clyde's arguments. Miss Clyde had undoubtedly sound ideas on the up-bringing of the young, and any amount of New England thrift. He had unlimited respect for her strength of character; but also his opinion as to why she was still *Miss* Clyde. "Maybe I've a queer mental twist," he went on audibly, "but that's just what I don't see the need of. Poor folk have to worry about making ends meet; but if money is of any use at all it's to save one that kind of fretting. When one feels the 'responsibility of wealth,' then it's a burden. I'd hate to think Blue Bonnet would ever get to that pass."

Mrs. Clyde wished for Lucinda just at this moment; Miss

C. E. Jacobs & Edyth Ellerbeck Read

Clyde could have met this argument with a worthy rejoinder, she was confident. "Don't you fear that thoughtless spending now may grow into future extravagance?" she asked rather helplessly.

"When the little girl begins to worry about bird-of-paradise aigrettes and pearl pendants for herself, I'll believe she's extravagant. As long as she spends only what she can afford and bestows it all upon others, I'll not begin to fret," he said decidedly.

"Then you don't think this camping-trip an extravagance? She is doing so much for the girls already that it seems rather unnecessary to me."

"It will be a wonderful experience for the girls—and they're just the right age to enjoy it most. A few years later they'll fuss about dirt and want springs on their beds."

Grandmother Clyde smothered a sigh; she had reached the latter stage, but perhaps it was not her place to "reason why." The conversation ended for the present, and during her stay on the ranch was not resumed.

As Uncle Cliff left the veranda after the conference, he was set upon by Blue Bonnet and Kitty and enticed to the lair of the We are Sevens, which chanced this time to be the summer-house in the Senorita's little garden. This rather shaky bower, overgrown by jack-beans which held together the would-be rustic structure, had once been the pride of Blue Bonnet's heart, but now, neglected—as was the garden since the advent of the ranch party—had become the residence of a large and growing family of insects. It served, however, as a very excellent spot for secret sessions such as the present one. A circular bench, very wobbly as to legs, had the advantage of bringing all the members face to face in solemn conclave. It was here their captive was haled.

"What says the noble Senora?" demanded Blue Bonnet, and then before he could answer she exclaimed—"Uncle Cliff, you must help us out. Life without that camping trip will be stale, flat and unprofitable."

"Oh, Blue Bonnet," said Sarah reproachfully, "how can you say that when we are having the most wonderful time that ever was?"

"Sarah, don't weaken our case," Blue Bonnet admonished her. "It's your place to look positively *pining*!"

"If you'll allow me to speak," remarked Uncle Cliff, "I'll put an end to your suspense. The Queen Mother says she will sacrifice herself for the weal of her subjects."

"Hooray!" cried Blue Bonnet, and the cry was echoed even by Sarah.

Alec and Knight, hearing the uproar on their way to the house, stopped and begged permission to enter.

"Come right in and sit down on the floor," said Blue Bonnet cordially. "Alec, Grandmother says she'll go!"

"So that's what all the row's about?" asked Knight. "Say, but I'm glad!"

Alec's eyes shone. "Don't you think I'd better go ahead with Knight? I could pick out a camping place and have everything ready for you." He had been awaiting a favorable moment to bring forth his quietly laid scheme, and the present seemed auspicious.

"I think that would be splendid," cried Blue Bonnet enthusiastically, reading Alec like a book. "But you'll wait and go with us, won't you, Uncle?"

"Can't go this trip. Pete has gone up with some of the boys to cut out a bunch of beef-cattle. I'll have to see to shipping them."

"Oh, Uncle,—we need you," remonstrated Blue Bonnet.

"And it's almost as good to be needed as it is to be wanted. Thank you."

"We want you even more than we need you," she insisted.

"You'll have plenty of men creatures to tyrannize over in camp. How many boys did you say there were, Knight?"

"There are twelve—and they know how to work, too."

"They'll be worked all right," said Uncle Cliff with a wicked twinkle.

"We must all work," said Sarah conscientiously. "I think we had better begin to plan things and get ready right away."

"The first thing to do," said Blue Bonnet, "is to make a huge lot of pinoche."

Sarah regarded her in astonishment. "Do you propose to live on pinoche?"

"No, goose, but with twelve boys in camp—not counting Alec and Knight, a pound won't go very far. And we must send to Jonah for marshmallows."

"Hadn't you better include several tons of angel-cake and fifty gallons or so of ice-cream?" asked Kitty.

"Just you wait, Kitty-Kat. When you see the use to which I put those marshmallows, you'll see that I'm the most practical member of the Club," Blue Bonnet prophesied solemnly.

"Grandmother, you're such a success," she said later, as they two sat discussing ways and means for the camping-trip.

"A success?" Mrs. Clyde questioned.

"As a grandmother, you know. If I'd had you made to order I wouldn't have had you a mite different! I hope our trip isn't going to be too hard for you. I promised Aunt Lucinda to take care of you, and I suspect sometimes that I'm not quite living up to the contract."

"We elderly people must guard against getting 'set in our ways.' Camp-life is certainly a good corrective for that." Mrs. Clyde smiled rather ruefully.

"It surely is," Blue Bonnet laughed. "It would never suit Aunt Lucinda. But she isn't sixty-five years young!"

"Nor fifteen years old."

"Was she ever? Somehow I can't imagine her different. It must give one a very—solid feeling, to be as sure about everything as Aunt Lucinda is. But she misses a lot of fun!"

Early the next morning Alec and Knight rode away; Knight looking very soldierly and capable now that his arm no longer reposed in its scarlet sling; Alec with his blankets in a business-like roll behind his saddle, and both boys provided with a "snack of lunch" to eat on the way. Alec's eyes were shining with anticipation; even Strawberry pranced more joyously than usual as though she knew a good time was in store.

The We are Sevens accompanied the travellers as far as Kooch's, and sent them off from that point weighted with injunctions and messages innumerable. That ride, even Sarah admitted, was a "grand and glorious" success; the air was fresh and sweet, Comanche very tractable, and everybody in the best of humors. The girls returned to the ranch full of plans for the camping trip, and for the rest of the day, and for several days following, made out exhaustive lists of eatables, bedding and utensils such as would have provided amply for a regiment of soldiers. In the midst of the preparations Sarah was caught red-handed packing her drawn-work among her effects.

"She'll have to be watched, girls," said Kitty. "White linen drawn-work on a camping-trip! Next she'll be slipping in white pique skirts and dancing slippers."

"I suppose you'll object to my taking handkerchiefs, too?" Sarah's look was a mixture of irony and indignation.

"We ought really to bar all hankies except bandanas," said Blue Bonnet, "but we'll stretch a point for Sarah's sake. She can't help having aristocratic tastes, you know."

Sarah was secretly of the opinion that drawn-work was no more out of place than the many boxes of pinoche and marshmallows that Blue Bonnet packed away in the huge "grub-boxes," but she yielded with her usual good grace.

By Wednesday all was pronounced in readiness for the start. Miguel was sent ahead with tents and supplies in one of the big cook-wagons used on the round-ups; with help from Alec and Knight he was to have a camp ready for the rest of the party when they should arrive on the following day.

"I wish Grandmother were not so set on the 'simple life,'" remarked Blue Bonnet, "for I should like to take Juanita along. It's a pity to separate her and Miguel just now, when things are progressing so nicely."

"How do you know?" Kitty looked up quickly.

Blue Bonnet bit her lip. She and Alec had agreed not to tell of the incident of the lasso, and she had kept the secret, though she burned to tell the romance-loving We are Sevens. "Just by signs," she answered evasively.

But Kitty could read signs, too, and privately longed to shake the mystery out of her hostess. Suspecting the trend of little Miss Why's thoughts, Blue Bonnet went on hurriedly: "How shall we go—in the buckboard or on horse-back?"

"Horse-back!" exclaimed all four of the others.

"Did I hear you speak, Sarah?" Kitty inquired.

"You did if you were listening," replied Sarah calmly.

"I believe Sarah and Comanche have formed a real attachment for each other," said Blue Bonnet who secretly exulted in Sarah's growing spirit.

"It must be a patent attachment then," laughed Kitty, "—something that keeps Sarah on!"

"Grandmother will have to go in the buckboard—Uncle Joe's going to drive and—" Blue Bonnet did some hasty calculating, "I had better stay with Grandmother—it's smoother riding with two in a seat. Firefly will hate being led, but I reckon some disciplining won't hurt him."

They were up before dawn in order to complete the first stage of the journey before noon. As they gathered about the lamp-lighted table for breakfast, yawning and rubbing their eyes, Blue Bonnet gave an amused laugh.

"'In *summer* I get up at night
And dress by yellow candle-light.'"

she quoted.

"I think it would have been a good plan to have had breakfast before we went to bed," said Sarah. "Thank you, Mrs. Clyde, I will take coffee, I think it will wake me up."

"Never mind," said Blue Bonnet. "You can just alter the lines a bit—

"'In camp it's quite the other way,
We'll all go straight to bed by day'—

and make up for the loss of our beauty sleep. And you'll see something worth getting up for later. Sunrise on the prairie, Kitty, makes the Massachusetts article look like your pink lawn when it came back from the wash."

They were several miles from the ranch when Uncle Joe raised his quirt and pointed to the east. "There she comes!" he warned.

The whole crowd came to a standstill in the middle of the road in a hush that was almost reverent. Blue Bonnet drew a deep breath. The rolling prairie with the long grass stirred by the breeze; the peaceful herds just waking into life; the fleecy clouds glowing from buff to rosy pink—she loved it all.

At eleven every one was ravenous and a halt was made for lunch. From that point the journey was hardly so pleasant; the road began to ascend sharply into the sturdy little range of hills that Texans proudly call mountains, and being less frequented than the county road, was rough and full of surprises in the way of snakes and insects. Sarah was just beginning to wonder if she could survive Comanche's next fright, when a loud "Whoa-o-o-pe!" sounded from somewhere above and ahead of them. Blue Bonnet answered immediately with the ranch-call which she and some of the cowboys had adapted years ago from one of Uncle Joe's old-time songs:

She had a strong, carrying voice, and the cheery summons of the Twickenham ferryman rang clearly on the air.

The next minute three riders emerged from the trees in whose shade they had been waiting, and galloped to meet the campers.

"It's Alec and Knight," Kitty called from the front. "And there's a girl with them!"

Blue Bonnet shot a quick glance at the approaching trio, and then gave a bounce of delight. That erect little figure, just about her own size, with the two pig-tails flying out behind her as she rode, could be no other than—Carita Judson.

Carita was not so quick at discovering her unknown friend; she gave a bashful, inquiring look at each one of the girls in turn. But as soon as she met Blue Bonnet's eye, full of an eager welcome, she rode straight to the side of the buckboard

C. E. Jacobs & Edyth Ellerbeck Read

and held out a slim, brown hand. "You are—you must be—a Texas Blue Bonnet!"

"And you're Carita,—I'm so glad!" Blue Bonnet took the outstretched hand in both her own and gazed with frank pleasure into the girl's smiling face.

Knight came up beside them and presented his cousin to Mrs. Clyde and the other girls, and after a short but merry halt they prepared to move on. Camp was still at some distance and they must get settled before nightfall.

Sarah came up to the buckboard just as the others were starting. "Do you mind changing places with me, Blue Bonnet?" she asked. "I'm tired of riding."

The look Blue Bonnet gave her was ample reward for what Sarah feared was almost an untruth on her part. She scrambled out of the saddle in a manner that Blue Bonnet would have smiled at ordinarily, but now regarded with sober eyes. The other girls, without giving a thought to her natural wish for a few words with Carita had ridden on in a gay whirl of conversation; Sarah with a thoughtfulness that Blue Bonnet was beginning to believe unfailing, had been the only one to read her unspoken wish.

"Isn't Sarah the dearest?" she whispered to her grandmother.

And Mrs. Clyde, mindful of a former comment of Blue Bonnet's, smiled with amusement as she replied—"Not half bad—considering her bringing-up!"

Carita had lingered behind the others and now as she saw Blue Bonnet mount Comanche, she rode back and joined her. They were the last of the procession and practically alone.

"It's so wonderful," Carita's small dark face was alight with pleasure, "—to think of seeing you after—everything!"

They smiled into each other's eyes. Carita did not in the least resemble the Woodford girls. She wore a queer one-piece garment of blue denim, not designed for riding, which pulled up in a bunch on either side of the saddle, showing her feet in thick boyish boots, and an inch or two of much-darned stocking. On her head was an old felt sombrero, sadly drooping as to brim and dented as to crown, secured under her chin by a piece of black elastic. Below it her small face, brown and freckled as it was, was not without a singular attraction. Her eyes were big and soft, her lips scarlet as holly-berries; and the long braids were very heavy and of a glossy chestnut. In spite of her clumsy costume she rode her wiry little pinto as Western girls ride—thistle-down in the saddle. She was a bit of the prairie herself, and Blue Bonnet saw it and loved her.

"When did you come?" Blue Bonnet asked her.

"Yesterday. And we're to stay over Sunday. Won't we just have to cram the days full?" Carita's eyes were wistful. "For fear we sha'n't have much time alone, I want to tell you how much it has meant to me—your letters, and the dress and the Christmas box and everything. I can't begin to tell you the—difference they have made. We've always had boxes you know—father has no regular salary. But nothing ever came that was half so wonderful. Last winter wasn't a bit like others—it was full of excitement!"

Blue Bonnet smiled, but she felt nearer tears than laughter. Such a little thing to mean so much! For the second time she had a feeling of thankfulness that she was—not poor. Money was certainly worth while when it could give such pleasure. If Miss Lucinda could have read the girl's mind at this moment, she might have felt some doubts as to her niece's ability to profit by the last winter's lesson in New England thrift. Blue Bonnet's only regret was that her purse which had been slipped into the missionary box, had not contained several times as much!

"I was sure we'd know each other, some day—I felt it!" Carita went on in her eager way. "And I believe Knight's meeting you that day was providential!"

"It was certainly providential for Sarah and me," Blue Bonnet laughed. "We'd have had a pretty spill if it hadn't been for him. But as 'all's well that ends well,' we can consider that everything has been for the best."

"That sounds like father." It seemed to Blue Bonnet that Carita smothered a sigh. "Mother and I aren't always sure that *everything* is for the best. But father never has the least bit of doubt." Then with a quick return of animation—"I know you'll love the camp. Knight has picked out the loveliest spot for your tents. There—look! You can see the Spring, and that gleam of white through the trees—that's Camp Judson!"

CHAPTER XI

CAMPING BY THE BIG SPRING

"OH, Blue Bonnet, do hurry!" cried Debby as Blue Bonnet galloped into camp. "It's the most wonderful place,—we can't wait for you to see it."

Blue Bonnet slipped from the saddle and flung the reins to Miguel.

"Show me everything!" she cried; and then not waiting to be shown, went from one tent to another in her usual whirlwind fashion.

"Our sleeping-tent," said Kitty; they were all trooping after the late-comer, chattering busily and explaining the most obvious arrangements. "That one's for you and the Senora; this one is the dining-room—see the table and benches Alec and Knight made! The kitchen is under that awning. Isn't that the darlingest stove?"

"And the little creek right handy!"

By the time she had completed her survey, Blue Bonnet was more enthusiastic than any one else. How she loved camping out!

C. E. Jacobs & Edyth Ellerbeck Read

The spot the boys had chosen for them was a beautiful one. Under two giant live-oaks whose branches interlaced overhead in a leafy canopy, the sleeping-tents were pitched, between them stretching an awning that formed both a dining-room and a lounging-place by day. The site had been used as a camping-ground before and still retained many conveniences installed by former campers; the underbrush had all been cut away, and the ground packed hard and level. For the kitchen, a canvas stretched between the camp-wagon and a convenient sycamore served as sufficient protection from sun and arboreal insects. The little sheet-iron stove, set up on a flat boulder, boasted an elbow in its pipe that could be adjusted to suit the direction of the wind.

A thread of a creek, tumbling down the hillside, ran not ten yards from the wagon, and at one point a tiny wooden trough had been inserted, giving the effect of a spout where kettles could be quickly filled. Alec and Knight had labored diligently to have all attractive as well as convenient, and really deserved great praise for the completeness of all details.

"Everything is perfect!" Blue Bonnet declared. "But we must have the buckboard seats in the—er—living-room. Uncle Cliff sent all three so that we could use them as easy chairs,—especially for Grandmo—why, where is she?"

"Here, dear," Mrs. Clyde came up with a tin dipper in her hand. "I've been having a drink,—such a drink, Blue Bonnet!" She held out the dripping cup and Blue Bonnet drank from it thirstily.

As she finished she met the Senora's eyes over the brim. "Oh, Grandmother, I ought to have done that—for you!" She shook her head. "I wonder if I'll ever think in time?"

Mrs. Clyde smiled and pushed the hair back from the girl's hot brow. "Where is Carita?"

"She rode on to tell her mother we had arrived. She'll be over later." Blue Bonnet glanced around the group. Every one looked warm, dusty, tired. And there was supper to get and beds to make! "What shall we do first, Grandmother?" Her manner was not exactly eager.

"First, we must all wash and brush up, for we are invited out to dinner!" Mrs. Clyde departed to suit the action to the words.

"Invited out—?" Blue Bonnet gazed at the girls incredulously.

"The boys of Camp Judson, represented by Knight, have invited us over there—"

"And we didn't waste any time in accepting!"

"Wasn't it thoughtful of them?" Blue Bonnet beamed on every one. "Now aren't you glad we brought the pinoche?"

"Let's go and dress," Debby urged.

"Dress?" echoed Blue Bonnet. "What are you going to wear—your pink panne velvet or your yellow chiffon?"

"Why, Blue Bonnet," said Sarah, "you know we haven't any clothes with us but these!"

Blue Bonnet groaned. "Then why is that worldly-minded Debby talking about dressing for dinner?"

"I meant wash and comb our hair," Debby protested.

"Where's the wash-basin, Blue Bonnet? I saw you with it when we were packing," said Sarah.

Blue Bonnet clapped a hand to her brow. "I think I put it in with the frying-pan."

"Are you sure it isn't in the bread-box?" Kitty asked.

"I wouldn't be sure it isn't." Blue Bonnet began a hasty search in the camp-wagon. Box after box was rummaged through, utensil after utensil picked up hopefully, only to disappoint when brought to the surface.

"There's no help for it," declared Debby, "we'll have to go and wash in the creek."

"Why, there may be campers below," said Sarah in a shocked tone, "and they wouldn't like to—"

"You needn't draw a diagram, Sarah," interrupted Blue Bonnet. "A word to the wise, you know. I'll polish off with cold cream." And she vanished.

Sarah, armed with towel and soap emerged from her tent a few minutes later and made her way through the willows to the creek. Blue Bonnet spying her called tauntingly: "Campers below!"

"I'm only going to wet one corner," Sarah went on calmly.

"Which corner—northeast or southwest?"

"Of the towel, of course." Then a minute later she called, "Girls, come quick!"

There was an immediate stampede to the creek.

"What is it—lions?" asked Amanda.

Sarah pointed without speaking. There, bending over an old tree-stump, admirably fashioned for a wash-stand, was the Senora calmly washing herself—in the basin.

"I found it here all ready for us," she explained. "And see— here's a nail on this little tree ready for a mirror, and branches just made to hang towels on."

"Alec and Knight haven't left a thing for me to see to," remarked Blue Bonnet. "I'm going to stop worrying."

"Oh, you were worrying, were you?" asked Kitty. "We'll know the symptoms next time."

The washing-up that ensued was very animated, if not thorough. Taking turns at the basin the girls, wincing under the cold water, "polished off" the top layer of dust; brushed ruffled locks and retied ribbons; dabbed talcum on noses and straightened creased middies. They were just putting on the finishing touches when the sound of cow-bells, rung lustily and long, came from the direction of the other Camp.

"That must be the dinner-bell," said Blue Bonnet. "I hope they won't expect us to have dainty appetites just because we're girls!"

A moment later Alec and Knight appeared to escort them in state. Midway they were met by Mr. and Mrs. Judson,—the latter with two small boys tugging at her skirts, and a third not far in the rear; a state of things that was later found to be invariably the case whenever Mrs. Judson ventured forth.

Blue Bonnet decided that she was going to like the whole Judson family. She liked the Reverend Mr. Judson with his delicate face and kind, nearsighted eyes. She liked him particularly because he looked so unministerial in his soft shirt and blue overalls. She liked Mrs. Judson, with her sweet, tired face looking out from a cavernous sun-bonnet. Mrs. Clyde's discerning eye read in the patient worn face a history of privation and self-denial; and surmised that the enthusiasm of the missionary was paid for most dearly by this uncomplaining partner.

It was to the tiniest toddler that Blue Bonnet was drawn most of all; she adored babies, and this chubby two-year-old was irresistible. She held out her arms to little Joe, but, to her surprise, he held off shyly. He scanned the row of ingratiating faces slowly, and not until his eyes rested on the kindly round countenance of Sarah did he show any response.

"Pitty lady!" he cried, holding out his arms and making a charge at her.

Sarah's face flushed pink with surprise and pleasure; and then with a rush she gathered Joe in a close hug. She had not realized until then how she had missed the little clinging arms at home.

"He spurns you, Blue Bonnet!" gasped Kitty.

"I reckon he can tell who has had experience with babies," Blue Bonnet remarked. The glance she gave Sarah was almost envious. "Well, pitty lady," she said at length, "you might leave a few kisses for somebody else!"

But Joe was chary and clung tightly to the lady of his choice; while the other girls secretly marvelled at any one's preferring Sarah to Blue Bonnet.

Carita made up for her brother's lack of appreciation; running to meet the girls, she drew Blue Bonnet's arm through her own and gave it an affectionate squeeze every few minutes.

"I hope the other girls won't mind if I monopolize you a little bit," she whispered; "they've had you so long and I'm to have such a short time."

This sort of incense no one could have been proof against; and Blue Bonnet was presently glowing.

"Welcome to Camp Judson!" said Knight proudly, as they neared a second grove of trees.

"Oh, how lovely!" Every one came to a standstill while they took in the pretty scene.

A model camp was Camp Judson. On a high flat knoll to the right was a long row of tiny white tents placed with military precision at regular spaces from each other, and each surrounded by a narrow trench. Among the trees gleamed other tents, and occasionally a gay quilt hung to air. Under one huge oak was the dining-room with a red-white-and-blue awning for a roof. Here were two long tables made of smooth boards laid on barrels, with rude benches running their entire length. They were guiltless of cloth and spread with tin dishes, for simplicity was a law as well as a necessity in this Camp. But a rustic basket of graceful ferns adorned one table, and the sun, hanging low in the sky, threw a pattern of quivering light and shade on the bare boards.

The girls had rather dreaded having to meet a dozen boys all at once. But they found the ordeal not half so bad as they had expected. The youngest boys were already gathered about the smaller table awaiting the signal to be seated; while the second table was reserved for the Judsons and their guests.

C. E. Jacobs & Edyth Ellerbeck Read

Standing beside it were three tall lads wearing towels pinned about them for aprons.

"Smith, Brown and Jones—the three props of the world!" explained Knight, with a wave of his hand; and the girls acknowledged the introduction without knowing which was which. "Keep your eye on the waiters, ladies and gentlemen," Knight continued, "and report all incivilities to the management. There's a fine for every cup of cocoa they spill down anybody's neck, and another for every spider they don't see first!"

Everybody stood beside the benches for a moment while Dr. Judson said a simple grace. Blue Bonnet noticed that even the smallest boy there bent his head at once, without even so much as a nudge from his neighbor. There was a second of absolute quiet after the pleasant voice finished the short invocation; then a shoving of benches, a rattle of dishes; and the meal progressed amid peals of laughter and an incessant clucking as of chickens at feeding-time.

"Talk about chattering girls!" Blue Bonnet challenged Alec with an amused glance. She found herself seated between him and Knight, an arrangement that suited all three admirably; while Carita smiled at her across the narrow table. Some of the older boys were beside Kitty, Debby and Amanda, and all three girls seemed to be well entertained. Sarah, with a small Judson on either side of her, was occupied chiefly in alternately kissing and feeding the youthful pair. Steaming *frijoles* in a huge earthen bowl; bass from the Spring, fried with slices of bacon; baked potatoes, cocoa and doughnuts formed the menu, which the hearty appetites of all transformed into a banquet; and no one felt compelled to refuse a second or third helping from motives of politeness.

"Where's the Spring?" Blue Bonnet asked suddenly. "The only creek I've seen is about as wide as my hand."

"Just a short walk from camp," Knight replied. "I'm saving that to show you in the morning."

There fell a moment of silence.

"Did I hear you sigh?" Alec was looking at Blue Bonnet in astonishment. She had never looked happier or prettier in her life; sun and wind had painted a rose-blush on her cheeks; the blue eyes were positively luminous. Yet he had distinctly heard her sigh.

She nodded. "I had to. I'm just too full for utterance—no, no!—I'll take another doughnut! I didn't mean that literally. But I'm full of content,—I'd like to purr."

Alec laughed. "It's the best fun I've ever had. I believe I must be part Indian, and this is the only time I've ever been able to obey 'the call of the wild.' It makes me sorry for all the misguided folk that spend all their lives in houses."

"Look at Grandmother," Blue Bonnet whispered. "Who would ever have thought that a Colonial Dame would look so natural eating beans with a tin spoon? I wish Uncle Cliff could have come, he's a born camper."

"Why didn't Mr. Terry come to dinner?" Knight asked.

"Uncle Joe!" Blue Bonnet's spoon dropped with a clatter. She hadn't even thought of Uncle Joe! "Mrs. Judson," she stammered, "will you please excuse me? I'll be right back." Hardly waiting for Mrs. Judson's surprised "Certainly," she sprang lightly over the bench and vanished through the trees.

The We are Sevens, used to Blue Bonnet's methods, went on unconcernedly with their dessert; but the Judsons looked mildly amazed.

Blue Bonnet found Uncle Joe smoking contentedly before a cosy gypsy fire on which a coffee-pot was steaming. She burst upon him breathlessly.

"Uncle Joe—I forgot,—you're invited out to dinner!"

He smiled at her over his pipe. "I ain't got a dinner-coat, Honey."

"But, Uncle Joe—it was horrid of me I know—"

"No uncomplimentary remarks, please," he interrupted; then seeing that she was really distressed he went on seriously: "Don't you worry about Uncle Joe, Blue Bonnet. He's used to looking out for Number One. I had to help Miguel hobble the horses, and that's a job that won't wait for any man. Now I've got tortillas and bacon and coffee, and I'm that comfortable I wouldn't stir for a whole company of Texas Rangers!"

As she reluctantly departed Uncle Joe looked after the slim figure with quiet delight. "Same old Blue Bonnet. Boston folks can't get any high-toned notions into that little head!"

As Blue Bonnet slipped back into her place, she found an animated discussion in progress.

"We're trying to decide on a name for our camp," Debby explained.

"We've run through Ashe, Clyde, Trent and the rest, but they're too—exclusive," said Kitty. "We want one that will include everybody."

"Why not 'Camp We are Seven?'" asked Knight.

"Too clumsy," declared Blue Bonnet.

"Use initials then," urged Knight.

"Camp W. A. S.—sounds rather like a has-been," remarked the bright-faced boy beside Kitty.

Blue Bonnet flashed him an appreciative smile. "That would never do for a crowd as—ahem—up-to-date as we try to be!"

"Let's have something beautiful," said Kitty.

"And romantic," added Debby.

"If you want something typical of this country," Dr. Judson spoke up, "—there's an expressive phrase often used here-abouts. Those of you who know the habits of the 'greasers' don't need to be told why their country is called the 'land of *poco tiempo*.' It means literally 'little time'—but with the Mexicans it usually means 'after a while' or even 'by and by.' 'Always put off till to-morrow what should be done to-day' is their version of our old motto."

"That just suits me!" cried Blue Bonnet.

"I love Spanish names," exclaimed Kitty.

Poco Tiempo the camp was straightway christened; and, as they later proved, its inmates had no difficulty in living up to the name.

CHAPTER XII

POCO TIEMPO

"I RECKON we'll all sleep without rocking," Blue Bonnet smiled drowsily in on the girls who were disrobing for the night. She had stolen from Grandmother's tent for a last word, but lingered for several before departing. "How's your bed, Sarah?"

"A bit bumpy," the honest girl admitted.

"Mustn't mind a little thing like that," Blue Bonnet admonished her.

"They're not very little—just you wait and see." Sarah squirmed about seeking a level spot for her body.

Alec and Knight, who had spent hours stuffing the bed-ticks with Spanish moss, would hardly have felt repaid could they have seen her discomfort at that moment.

Observing her Blue Bonnet remarked: "I'm glad we brought the canvas cot for Grandmother. I don't mind bumpy beds myself—it isn't right to be too comfortable when you're camping out."

Kitty stood, mirror in hand, ministering unto a blistered nose, and as Sarah gave a final grunt before closing her eyes, she called suddenly: "Sarah Blake, don't you dare go to sleep 'til we've drawn lots."

"Lots?" Sarah blinked sleepily.

"To see who's to get breakfast. After that we'll take turns, two at a time."

"But there are five of us," protested Debby.

"Grandmother says to count her in. We'll give her Sarah for a running-mate,—she's about the only one that can keep Sallykins in order."

Sarah woke up at that to give the speaker a surprised and grieved look, at which Blue Bonnet burst into a laugh. "I'll label my next joke, Old Reliable," she said.

Kitty looked about her for something which they could use for lots.

Nothing seeming appropriate, she suddenly tweaked three bright hairs from her own curly head, arranged them in lengths and held them out for the others to draw.

"Shortest gets breakfast; next lunch, longest dinner," she announced tersely.

"Hooray for us!" cried Amanda, catching Blue Bonnet around the waist and hopping about on one foot, the other being unshod. "Lunch for us. Let's think up something easy."

Kitty made a grimace at the short hair left in her hand. "Breakfast! Debby, I call that hard luck."

"The others may call it harder," prophesied Blue Bonnet.

"Never mind, the Senora and Sarah will make up for it at dinner-time," said Kitty.

"Night-night!" said Blue Bonnet, preparing to leave. With her hand on the tent-flap she paused. "Shake out your shoes before you put them on in the morning!" she said; and with this dark warning fled.

Camp Judson had awakened, had had a fiercely contested water-fight, had breakfasted, tidied up, and most of its inmates scattered in quest of adventures, before the tired girls of *Poco Tiempo* gathered for the morning meal. Kitty and Debby, enveloped in capacious gingham aprons, and appearing somewhat flushed and nervous, stood waiting to serve.

Mrs. Clyde gave the two cooks an approving smile. "Everything looks charming," she said as she took her place at the head of the board.

The table here was spread with white oilcloth, and the dishes of blue enamelled-ware showed bright and cheerful against the immaculate expanse. Bowls of steaming oatmeal porridge stood at each place, and huge mugs of cocoa. But it was at none of these that Blue Bonnet was gazing; her eyes were fastened in wonder on a pitcher of real milk and another of real cream.

"Where did that come from?" she demanded.

"The Spring!" declared Kitty.

"Miguel rode to the Circle Y ranch and got it early this morning," Debby confessed, "and they're going to let us have it every morning."

"It's a jarring note," Blue Bonnet declared.

"All right, you can have all the 'condemned milk' you want," said Kitty, "—we've a dozen cans of it."

But Blue Bonnet was already helping herself generously to the "jarring note" and seemed to enjoy it as much as any one. Every one was exceedingly polite and made no mention of lumps in the porridge; and finally the anxious puckers in Debby's forehead began to smooth themselves out. There was a moment of veritable triumph for the cooks when they came in with the nicely browned bacon and a plate heaped high with golden corn-bread.

"Who was the artist?" the Senora asked in pleased surprise.

"I didn't know you knew how," Sarah commented.

There was a moment's hesitation, and then Blue Bonnet, who had caught a glimpse of Uncle Joe's face, pointed an accusing finger at him. "Fess up, Uncle Joe!"

Much annoyed at himself, Uncle Joe tried to deny the accusation, but Kitty's face confirmed the suspicion against him, and in the end he "fessed up" rather lamely.

"Have to do something to earn my board and keep," he protested.

"Amanda and I get lunch, you know," Blue Bonnet suggested tactfully; and Amanda telegraphed her approval of this gentle hint.

"Well, this camp is well-named," said Knight, appearing

suddenly with a half-dozen boys in his train. "Is this breakfast or lunch?"

"Breakfast, and a very good one," Mrs. Clyde remarked. "Won't you join us?"

"Don't tempt my merry men," Knight begged comically. "They've never yet been known to refuse food, and though it's only an hour since breakfast, I've no confidence in them."

"Won't you please hurry?" Alec asked eagerly. "I can't wait for you all to see the Spring."

"We're ready right now," said Blue Bonnet, jumping up impulsively. "Come on, girls, it's a glorious morning for a tramp."

"Haven't you forgotten something, Blue Bonnet?" her grandmother asked.

Blue Bonnet looked puzzled. "Do you mean hats? I'd much rather go without one, if you don't mind, Grandmother."

But it was not hats that Grandmother was thinking of; gradually it dawned on Blue Bonnet that the other girls were not making ready for the excursion, but were gathering up the dishes and clearing the table. She flashed a reproachful look at them.

"You might let those wait," she protested.

Grandmother smiled. "You do surely belong to the 'land of *poco tiempo*,' Blue Bonnet."

"But the dishes will keep—"

"And so will the Spring!"

The girl gave a discouraged sigh; it was a pity Grandmother had not been brought up in Texas; then she would have understood what were the really necessary things in life. She nodded wistfully at the boys. "Grandmother believes in every girl's doing her duty," she said.

"We'll have the manager hold the performance," said Knight cheerfully. "We'll be back in half an hour,—Carita can go by that time, too."

Blue Bonnet brightened visibly at this, and turned resolutely to the hated tasks.

"Debby and I will wash the dishes; Sarah can 'red up,' and you and Amanda do the beds," Kitty suggested.

Aunt Lucinda's training stood Blue Bonnet in good stead here. The going over the rather bumpy beds got in that half-hour left Amanda breathless with admiration.

"You can do things beautifully when you want to, Blue Bonnet," she remarked.

"When I have to, you mean," Blue Bonnet replied.

"Where's the broom, do you know?" asked Sarah.

"Sh!" Blue Bonnet drew her into the tent and out of every one's hearing. "There isn't any broom, Sarah."

"But I put one in the wagon myself."

"And I *threw it out!*"

"Blue Bonnet!" Something like horror was in Sarah's blue eyes.

Blue Bonnet met her gaze defiantly. "Did you ever see a picture of the Witch of Salem, Sarah?"

Sarah gave a bewildered nod. "What has the Witch of Salem—"

"Wasn't she riding a broom?" Blue Bonnet persisted.

"Yes—but—"

"Well, in my opinion that's the only good use a broom was ever put to! It has no place in a respectable camping party."

Sarah said no more; but when, a few minutes later, Amanda and Blue Bonnet looked out to learn the source of an odd sound, they beheld the indomitable Sarah, armed with an antiquated rake, gathering up the leaves and litter on the hard dirt "floor" of the dining-room.

"Who would have thought to see our Sarah grown rakish?" asked Blue Bonnet,—and then dodged the pillow sent by Amanda's indignant hand.

By the time the allotted half-hour was up, *Poco Tiempo* was a model of neatness and order. The girls, booted and hatted in spite of Blue Bonnet's objections, were ready to the minute, and when the young scouts appeared they set out at once, exactly—as Blue Bonnet remarked—like the third-graders at recess.

Grandmother had settled herself comfortably with a book,—Mrs. Judson was coming over later for a chat,—and so it was with a free mind and a soul ready for a carnival of pleasure that Blue Bonnet stepped forth on the joyous expedition.

"I reckon it is better," she admitted to Alec, "to have everything done first, instead of having them to do when you're tired."

"Oh, wise young judge!" he laughed. "We'll make a New Englander of you yet."

"That reminds me of something Cousin Tracey said once. He thought I was developing a New England conscience, and said it was an exceedingly troublesome thing to have around. I believe him,—it's much more fun to develop Kodak films. There now!" she broke off impatiently, "—if I haven't left my camera in the tent. And I want pictures of the Spring."

"Never mind, we'll be up here every day," said Alec. "There's a jolly little rustic bridge where you can gather the crowd for a group picture. Here we are!"

He and Blue Bonnet had walked faster than the others, and so were first to see this most beautiful of springs. Blue Bonnet gave one look, and then something rose in her throat, stifling breath and speech. Alec watched her appreciatively.

"If he speaks to me now, he's not the boy I've always believed him," the girl was saying to herself. She dreaded the first word that should break in on that moment of perfect beauty.

Below them the giant spring surged up, a great emerald in a setting of woods and hills. Clear as air, the water boiled up from the bowels of the earth, revealing every fish and pebble in its mirror-like depths. Shrubs overhung it; wild cresses and ferns clustered about it; below the surface long tresses of pinky-coral grasses floated and waved in the bubbling current.

A voice shattered the blissful moment of peace. "Isn't she a beauty?"

It was a sandy-haired youth with Kitty who had clambered roughly into the picture. Blue Bonnet hated him fiercely for a few seconds. Then the rest came up with a babble of voices and exclamations and she resigned herself, with a sigh, to the fact that the gift of silence, being golden, is given to but few.

Knight gave her a questioning glance and she glowed back at him. "It's perfect—almost too perfect."

"There's a wee spring up higher,—the camp creek flows from it. Do you feel equal to the climb?" he asked her.

She gave eager assent, and, after lingering a few minutes for the others and finding them too slow for the pace she liked, Blue Bonnet followed Knight up a steep winding path that circled the hill.

He carried a "twenty-two" rifle swung across his shoulders, and in his belt a rather formidable looking knife.

"For use or ornament?" she asked, indicating the weapons. "You look like Dick Danger."

"Strictly for use," he assured her. "The gun has brought down many a toothsome 'possum, and the knife serves to cut anything from firewood to alpenstocks. Shall I cut you one to assist your feeble steps?"

They halted while he selected a sapling for the purpose, trimmed and sharpened it at the end.

"Alpine travellers put sharp iron points on their staffs, Uncle says," he explained, "so that by thrusting them in the ice and snow they keep from slipping. We don't need them for just that purpose, but they are handy on steep paths—and to kill bugs with!"

She accepted the "alpenstock" gratefully and soon found it useful for both purposes.

"When we get back to camp I'll get Sandy to carve your initials in it—he's quite a genius at carving," Knight said.

"Is Sandy the—sandy one?"

"Precisely."

"Then I don't think I like him."

"Oh, but you will when you know him better," Knight protested. "He's tremendously clever,—a born orator. He won a medal last year in a debate."

"That accounts for his talking so much," Blue Bonnet laughed. "He's always at it."

"But unlike most incessant talkers, he says something," Knight urged for his friend. "We'll get him to recite some evening, then you can judge how talented he is."

"Does he do 'Curfew shall not—?'" she asked mischievously.

"Grief, no!" Knight's disgusted tone sent Blue Bonnet off in a fit of laughter. To her surprise the ripple of her laugh came back in a gleeful "ha, ha!" that had something witchlike about it. She turned a startled face to her companion.

"We've reached the 'Whispering Grotto,'" he explained. "The echo is famous." He pushed aside a low-growing bough, and

148   C. E. Jacobs & Edyth Ellerbeck Read

brushing by it Blue Bonnet found herself in a lovely little cave-like spot, in the centre of which was a tiny spring. It bubbled up somewhere back in the hill and had made a long tunnel, coming to the light just here.

"Oh, for a cup. I'm thirsty as—as Tantalus!" sighed Blue Bonnet.

"A Texas girl crying for a cup?" Knight asked teasingly.

"That wouldn't have happened before I went to Woodford. I've been going through what they call—being civilized. It's mostly learning not to shock the New England sense of propriety."

"I'm not a New Englander!"

Knight's eyes were daring her; and it was fatal. What Sarah would have said if she could have seen Blue Bonnet's method of getting a drink is hard to conjecture. Hardly had she time to spring to her feet when voices were heard close at hand.

"I can hear Sandy." She turned eagerly to Knight. "Let's go on—I don't feel ready for a crowd."

"There's a lovely view from the top of the hill," he suggested.

Her only answer was to push on, plying her alpenstock eagerly in her haste to elude the others. Pausing only when the top of the hill was reached, she sank at length on a fallen tree-trunk. The view was all Knight had promised for it, overlooking a quiet valley.

"Let's call it 'Peaceful Valley,'" she said.

"It may have a different name on the map, but no one can

prevent our christening it what we like," he agreed.

Blue Bonnet was content to rest for a while here. There was no sign of life anywhere, except a solitary bird wheeling about far above their heads.

"A swallow-tailed kite," Knight said as the bird dropped suddenly into clearer view. "Graceful, isn't it?"

All at once the big kite alighted on the dead branch of a tree near them.

"What glorious wings!" breathed Blue Bonnet.

"Would you like one for your hat?" Knight asked.

"Oh, wouldn't I!" she cried eagerly.

Quick as flash Knight swung his rifle about, aimed and fired. Blue Bonnet put her fingers in her ears with an exclamation of alarm. The bird toppled as if to fall, then righted itself with a lurch and fluttered out from the tree. Blue Bonnet gave a sigh of relief.

"I was so afraid you had hurt him!" she cried,—and the words died away in a gasp of distress. The kite, pitching headlong, had fallen almost at her feet.

She dropped on her knees beside it; but the bird was still. Knight, bending over her, was suddenly filled with surprise and dismay; she was crying like a child.

"It was so mean and vain of me," she said with quivering lips, "—to want him just for a hat, when he was having such a beautiful time."

Knight was pale with hatred of himself.

She looked up at last and smiled mistily through her tears. "I reckon you think I am pretty much of a baby. But I can't bear to see things—die."

"It's only a big hawk," he said to comfort both himself and her.

She looked up hopefully. "And hawks are mean birds, aren't they,—that kill little chickens and other birds?"

He hesitated, then said unwillingly: "Some hawks do. But this is a different kind. It lives on snakes and insects—"

"Then it is a good bird!—that's what Uncle Cliff calls them." Her face clouded again and she turned towards camp.

"You don't want one of the wings then?"

She shuddered. "Oh, no!" Then she paused. "I will have—I saw some feathers fall. Will you give me one? I want it for a reminder."

Knight picked up one of the tiny barred wing-feathers and handed it to her. "A reminder?"

"I'm never going to wear things like that again—wings and birds and all those cruel ornaments. I never realized before— And whenever I am tempted I shall look at this."

Knight bent, picked up another of the feathers and laid it away in his fly-book. "I need a reminder, too," he remarked.

"But you never wear birds in your hats," Blue Bonnet

said wonderingly.

"My reminder shall be: 'Think before you shoot,'" he said quietly.

C. E. Jacobs & Edyth Ellerbeck Read

CHAPTER XIII

AROUND THE CAMP-FIRE

THERE was no sign of the other trampers when Blue Bonnet and Knight reached the little grotto; and descending to the Big Spring they found even that charming spot deserted.

Blue Bonnet looked around in surprise.

"Do you suppose we've missed them on the way down?" Raising her voice she gave her ranch-call—"Ho, ye ho, ho!"

"—ho ho!" the hill sent back; but no feminine or masculine voice answered the well-known notes.

Blue Bonnet, child of the open, then looked at the sun and the shadows and gave an exclamation of astonishment. "It's past noon! They've gone back to camp. My, I'll have to hurry—it's my turn to cook lunch."

She darted impetuously down the hillside, and Knight found himself compelled to move briskly in order to keep up with her. They went too fast for conversation, but once Blue Bonnet paused long enough to say over her shoulder— "You'll come to lunch, won't you?"

"Catch me refusing now I know who the cook is!" he replied gaily.

The path opened at last on the open space before *Poco Tiempo*. There was sound of voices and laughter, and yes— the clink of dishes! Blue Bonnet turned a rueful face to Knight—"Do you hear that? They won't say a thing to me!"

"I am armed,—trust me to protect you," he declaimed theatrically.

They had to pass through the "kitchen" first, and there the clutter of empty pots and pans told their own story. From the dining-room the others caught sight of the tardy pair and a wild hubbub at once arose.

"Tramps!"

"Set the dogs on them!"

"Why don't you work for a living?"

Knight's eyes twinkled as he looked from Blue Bonnet's amazed countenance to the teasing faces about the table. Lunch was evidently not only ready but largely consumed.

"What are you eating so early for?" Blue Bonnet demanded.

"Early!"

"Twenty minutes past one!"

"No—!" Blue Bonnet gasped, subsiding on the end of the bench and fanning her hot face with her hat. "Now, isn't that the funniest thing?"

"I'm glad you see the point of your own joke," retorted Kitty. "We have decided to give you a week's notice to get a new place."

"I engage her on the spot," said Knight. "It's all my fault."

"We won't give her a reference," said Kitty.

"You needn't—if you'll just give me food," said Blue Bonnet. "Alec, make room for Knight beside you, will you? We're both starved. Who made the muffins?"

"Guess," said Kitty, relenting and passing her the nearly empty plate.

Sarah intercepted it. "I'll get you some hot ones." And she rose hastily.

Blue Bonnet laughed. "Now I know! Grandmother, did you help Sarah?"

Mrs. Clyde nodded. "The girls came back so hungry I thought we had better not wait for the chief cook. No one knew where you were."

"I'm going to wear a cow-bell after this," Blue Bonnet declared. "Sarah, if I could make such muffins I'd insist upon cooking every meal."

"I reckon you don't need any protection," Knight said in an undertone.

"Oh, there's safety in numbers. Wait till Amanda catches me alone! We two will have to get dinner now." She buttered her third muffin and then glanced happily around the table. "I've a lovely scheme," she hinted.

"Did you ever see any one so bowed down with penitence?" asked Kitty; adding promptly, "What's the scheme?"

"It's to invite Alec and Knight to get down logs, make us a huge bonfire and—"

"That's just like Blue Bonnet," Kitty broke in, "—she'll let you do the work and she'll do the *rest*!"

"—and then invite them to a party," Blue Bonnet went on imperturbably.

"'She'll do the grand with a lavish hand,'" quoted Alec. "We're your men. A Party—with a big P—is what our souls have been pining for. Where shall we build the festive pyre?"

"In the open space between the two camps. There'll be no danger to the trees there and plenty of room to sit around it. I'll tell Miguel to bring up one of the wagon horses to drag logs,—I want a perfectly mammoth fire."

"You ought to have been a man, Blue Bonnet," Debby remarked, "—you would have made such a wonderful general. Your ability to put other people to work amounts to positive genius."

But Blue Bonnet had already gone in search of Miguel, with Alec and Knight in her train. For the rest of the afternoon the "General" demonstrated that she could not only put other people to work, but could work herself, to advantage. While the boys—whose forces had been augmented by the addition of Sandy, Smith, Brown and Jones—got down logs and built them into a miniature log cabin, Blue Bonnet made great preparations for the Party. She spread all her Indian blankets at a proper distance from the bonfire-to-be; distributed the buck-board seats judiciously, planning to add the dining-room benches as soon as supper was out of the way; whittled great quantities of long willow wands to a sharp point, maintaining great secrecy as to the use to which the latter were to be put; and stacked many boxes of the delectable pinoche in a convenient spot.

Hardly had these preparations been completed when Amanda announced that it was time to begin cooking dinner. Blue Bonnet looked at her aghast.

"I think it's maddening," she declared. "We are in a continual state of washing up after one meal and getting ready for another. And this is what Grandmother calls 'simplicity'—! It would be a heap—much—simpler if I could just say—'Lisa, we'll have dinner at six.' That would end it,—and what could be simpler?"

"What shall we have?" asked Amanda, considering that subject more to the point.

"Baked potatoes, then we won't have to peel them,—I'd as soon skin a rabbit. And Gertrudis cooked a leg of lamb, so that we'll only have to warm it up."

"Shall we try hot bread?" asked Amanda.

"Certainly not! Hot bread twice to-day already—we'll all have indigestion. We've stacks of loaves, and bread and maple syrup is good enough camp fare for any one. If we're going in for the simple life, let's be simple."

"That reminds me of something we translated in the German class," said Amanda. "'Man ist was er isst'—and it means 'one is what one eats.' And another German said 'Tell me what you eat and I'll tell you what you are.'"

"Do you mean to tell me that if I live on angel-cake I'll grow to be angelic?" demanded Blue Bonnet.

"Hardly!" laughed Amanda. "It would take a good deal more than that! No offence, Blue Bonnet,—I like you best when you're—the other thing. The Germans are always arguing about something or other. We used to take sides in class and nearly come to blows."

"You should have taken French," said Blue Bonnet, before she thought.

"You didn't think that last March!" Amanda teased; and the next moment could have bitten her tongue out for the thoughtless speech. Blue Bonnet did not smile; it was evident that the memory of the day when all the members of the French class except herself had "cut" was still a bitter one.

"I'll wash the potatoes," Amanda offered in amend for having touched a painful chord.

"All right!" Blue Bonnet beamed acceptance of the kind intention and handed over the pan without hesitation. "I'll make up a hot fire, and we'll get everything started and the table set,—then you and I are going to the Spring."

"Oh, are we?" asked Amanda blankly. One never knew what scheme lurked in the back of Blue Bonnet's head.

"For table decorations. I saw some ferns and wild honey-suckle near the bank, and it won't take much time to gather enough for the table."

"Decorating the table isn't 'simple,' is it?" Amanda asked rather provokingly.

"If you know anything simpler than a wildflower, I'd like to be shown it," retorted Blue Bonnet. "Come on, we must do some tall hustling."

The "tall hustling" got the table set in a rather sketchy fashion; hurried the potatoes into a scorching oven; placed the already cooked roast in the top of the same oven at the same time; and saw Blue Bonnet and Amanda headed for the Spring, bearing a fruit-jar and the camp's only carving-knife, just as Uncle Joe came up the bank with a fine string of speckled trout.

"All ready to fry, Honey," he said, holding them up proudly.

"Hide them quick!" cried Blue Bonnet in alarm, "shooing" him back towards the creek.

Used as he was to Blue Bonnet's impetuosity, this move of hers filled him with amazement. "What's the matter,—they're perfectly good trout!" he urged.

"They're lovely. But I wouldn't fry one for ten million dollars! Keep them for breakfast, Uncle Joe,—Sarah will know how to do them beautifully."

With an understanding chuckle, Uncle Joe went off to cache his string of beauties in a cool place along the creek; and Blue Bonnet and Amanda continued their quest for ferns.

As they were returning, crowned with success, they met the Senora just back from a stroll with Mrs. Judson. The three other girls were already sitting suggestively about the board.

"There," said Blue Bonnet triumphantly, as she deposited the fruit-jar in the centre of the table with its graceful ferns and honeysuckle trailing over the oil-cloth, "feast on that!"

"I call that a pretty slim dinner," said Kitty.

Blue Bonnet, disdaining the insinuation, departed rather hastily to the kitchen, drawn thither by a strong odor and a still stronger suspicion of disaster. The sheet-iron stove was red-hot. Catching up a cloth she flung open the oven door, and then backed abruptly away from the cloud of acrid yellow smoke that rolled thickly into her face.

"Oh, Blue Bonnet!" wailed Amanda. "Everything's burned to a cinder! We shouldn't have gone off."

Blue Bonnet's only reply was a violent fit of coughing. The smoke continued to pour in dense billows from the oven. "Grab the pans, quick!" she managed to choke out.

Amanda made a valiant dive through the smoke, and had just time to seize the pans from the top and bottom of the oven, when she, too, was overcome, and in the paroxysm of coughing that followed threatened to burst a blood-vessel. Finally with crimson faces and streaming eyes, both cooks gazed ruefully down on the black marbles that had been potatoes, and the charred drum-stick that had once been a leg of spring lamb.

"Keep back—no trespassing!" called Blue Bonnet as the other girls, scenting fun as well as the odor of burning things, came running from the dining-room. "This is our funeral and we don't want any mourners!" She waved them back peremptorily, at the same time screening the ruins with her apron.

The discomfited We are Sevens returned to their seats, and a moment later there came the sound of spoons being vigorously thumped on the table.

"We want dinner!" came imperiously from the hungry girls.

Amanda looked imploringly at her partner. "What shall we do?"

Blue Bonnet thought hard for a moment. All at once her brow cleared. "Here, take the meat, go find a gopher-hole and push that bone down into it as far as it will go. The potatoes can't be burned all the way through,—we'll scrape what's left into a bowl. And I'll tell Uncle Joe I've changed my mind,—we'll have the trout for dinner. And, Amanda, you'll hurry back, won't you, and put the fish in the pan—I simply can't touch 'em!"

Each sped to fulfil her allotted task, and in an incredibly short space of time a family of gophers was sniffing about a strange object blocking their front door; and a pan of fragrant trout sputtered on top of the little stove. As Blue Bonnet set the great platter of perfectly browned fish in front of her grandmother, there was a flattering "ah!" of anticipation that repaid—almost repaid, her for the previous bad quarter of an hour. Canned pears and the cookies that should have been saved for future emergencies, completed a dinner which was voted "not half bad" by the other girls, who secretly marvelled at getting any dinner at all. No one noticed that neither Blue Bonnet nor Amanda partook of potatoes, and there proved to be ample for the rest.

"I'll wash the dishes, Amanda," Blue Bonnet offered, when at last that night-mare of a dinner was over. "I ought to walk over red-hot plowshares, or wear a hair-shirt or something as a penance for my sins of this day. Lacking both plowshares and shirt, I'll substitute dish-washing. And you may bear me witness—I'd take the hair-shirt if I had my choice!"

It was a very weary Blue Bonnet who turned the dishpan

upside down and hung the dish-cloth on a bush to dry. The long tramp of the morning, the preparations for the bonfire party, and then the exhausting experience of getting dinner, had tired even her physique, which had seldom known fatigue.

"I wish we could dis-invite the company," she said to Amanda.

"So do I," groaned her partner. "Fancy having to sit around a bonfire and sing 'merrily we roll along'—! It makes me ache all over."

Later, when the inmates of both camps were gathered in a great circle about the fire, singing, jesting and story-telling, both girls forgot their weariness and might have been heard singing the same "merrily we roll along" with great zest and vocal strength.

The bonfire did its builders proud and without any preparatory sulking or coaxing burst almost at once into pillars of soaring flame. There was a backing away at first on the part of the spectators as the intense heat began to scorch the circle of faces; then a gradual drawing near again. It was not until the flames had died down and the logs were a mass of glowing coals that Blue Bonnet handed around her willow-wands. Each one was now tipped with a white ball, puffy, round and mysterious.

To most of the boys this was an innovation, and they had to be shown how to hold the white globules over the coals until they spluttered and swelled to bursting.

"Now eat them!" she commanded. There was a chary tasting and then an ecstatic cry—"Marshmallows!"

C. E. Jacobs & Edyth Ellerbeck Read

The rapidity with which the tin boxes were emptied might have appalled a less generous provider than Blue Bonnet; but she had relied upon Uncle Cliff to fill her order for marshmallows, and consequently felt no fear of "going short."

When little Bayard had consumed his ninth "moth-ball" as he persisted in calling the sweets, his mother rose to take her brood home. Mr. Judson bent to lift Joe who had fallen asleep in Sarah's arms, and then turned to Blue Bonnet. "Good-night," he said, holding out his free hand and smiling down into the girl's tired face; "this is the first time I ever partook of toasted moonshine, and I've enjoyed my initiation."

Carita kissed her impulsively. "It's the loveliest party I've ever been to," she whispered.

Blue Bonnet looked wistfully after the departing group. "Aren't families the nicest things in all the world?" she asked Sarah, as she sank on the blanket beside this member of a numerous clan.

"The very nicest." And Sarah, whose arms still felt the warmth of little Joe, stared into the fire with eyes that saw in the coals the picture of a family in far-off Woodford.

There were a few more songs; an eighth or ninth rendition of

"Meet me, dearest Mandy,
By the water-melion vine"—

for the benefit of Amanda, who hated it, and then the rest rose reluctantly to depart.

"It's the swellest thing in the bonfire line I've ever attended," Sandy assured Mrs. Clyde; and she could excuse the phrase because of the undoubted enthusiasm of the speaker.

Half a dozen of the boys tramped away in a bunch, and there floated back to the group about the fire the rhythmic refrain of "Good-night, ladies!" until it finally died away in a sleepy murmur.

Only the older boys had lingered and they, after making arrangements for a horse-back ride on the morrow, slowly straggled away.

"Where's Blue Bonnet?" asked Alec; he was one of the last, loitering for a final word with his hostess.

"She was sitting by me a little while ago," said Sarah, looking towards the Navajo.

The spot was in shadow, but as they looked in that direction, a log fell, and a slender flame sprang up. In the light they saw Blue Bonnet, curled up on the bright blanket, with her head pillowed on her arm.

She was fast asleep.

CHAPTER XIV

A FALLING IN

"HOW'S the Sleeping Beauty this morning?" was Alec's salutation to Blue Bonnet, when he appeared early next day in advance of the other picnickers. Blue Bonnet asleep at her own party had been a spectacle he would not soon forget; it was almost as funny as being absent from her first tea, on that memorable day in Woodford.

"The Sleeping Beauty could find it in her heart to envy Rip Van Winkle; a nap like his is just what I crave. But no,— Sarah must needs have breakfast at cock-crow," Blue Bonnet complained.

"Why, Blue Bonnet, it was after eight o'clock when I called you," returned Sarah in a grieved tone.

"Sarah didn't want breakfast mistaken for lunch again," said Amanda.

"My prophetic soul tells me that we are going to conduct ourselves like a model Sunday-school class to-day," Blue Bonnet remarked.

"What makes you think so?" asked Amanda, in whom the

memory of yesterday's trials was still undimmed.

"'Well begun is half done,' you know. And this beginning is obnoxiously perfect." Blue Bonnet was wiping off the oil-cloth as she spoke; dishes were already washed, beds done, and all without a hitch.

"I hope our picnic won't prove to be of the Sunday-school variety," said Kitty.

"I'm sure our Sunday-school picnics at home are always very nice," Sarah said reprovingly.

"Every one to his taste!" was Kitty's airy rejoinder.

"You can make up your mind that this picnic won't be like any other you ever attended," Alec assured them. "Knight has a scheme up his sleeve that will bear watching. I wonder, Blue Bonnet, if Mrs. Clyde would mind letting us take coffee?"

Blue Bonnet reflected. "To-morrow is Sunday and we're privileged to have it for breakfast. If we have it to-day instead I'm sure she won't object. What else shall we take?"

"Only some bread, some lump sugar and a tin of milk, please," said Alec modestly.

Amanda gave a sudden exclamation of joy. "Then we won't be back to lunch,—oh, Blue Bonnet, that lets us out to-day!"

They fell upon each other rapturously.

"I think we are the ones who should rejoice," said Kitty; but her remark met with the silent scorn it deserved.

They mustered a troop of twelve, all mounted, for Knight's picnic. Riding by twos, they cantered decorously as long as the eyes of their elders followed their course; but when a turn in the road freed them from observation, there was a spurring and an urging of the wiry ponies, and away they went, recking little of the grade whether up or down.

It became a game of follow-my-leader, with Knight and Blue Bonnet heading the procession and putting their horses through a performance that would have lamed anything but a Western cow-pony. Knight finally led the way to one of the "race-paths" that abound in the hilly regions of Texas, and there began a tournament that for years lived in Sarah's memory as the most reckless exhibition of daring ever seen outside a circus-ring.

"Who made this race-track?" she asked Knight in one of the infrequent pauses in the performance.

"Nature!" He laughed at the look of incredulity with which Sarah met this assertion. In truth she had good reason to doubt his word; the smooth broad road encircling the hill, a full quarter of a mile long, edged on either side by a dense growth of cedars, seemed unmistakably to show the hand of man in its creation.

"It's the solemn truth I'm telling you," Knight insisted, "—I swear it by the mane of my milk-white steed!"

Sarah gave one glance at the dark yellow buckskin pony he rode, and then clucked impatiently to Comanche. She objected to having her faith in people imposed upon.

Knight was still laughing when Blue Bonnet came up and challenged him to a race. "My reputation for truth-telling is forever lost in Senorita Blake's estimation," he told her.

"What do you think of Sarah, anyway?" It would be curious to know just how a Western boy regarded Old Reliable.

"She's very nice," he said, with an utter absence of enthusiasm, "—but not exciting."

Blue Bonnet smiled. "And Kitty?" she continued. Perhaps it wasn't polite in a hostess to discuss her guests, but she just had to ask that.

"She's very pretty and vivacious," he replied with an increase of warmth. "She lacks only one thing to make her irresistible."

"And that?"

"Having been brought up in Texas!"

If Knight had expected a blush to follow his outspoken compliment he was disappointed. Blue Bonnet's hearty laugh showed a very healthy absence of self-consciousness in her make-up.

"My Aunt Lucinda thinks that is my very worst drawback," she declared; and then chirping to Firefly, she was off at a break-neck pace, hat bobbing, brown braid flying, her eyes alight with the excitement of the race.

The climax of the day was the gypsy picnic. When Blue Bonnet beheld the camp-fire with the pail of coffee steaming away over the bed of coals, and saw the feast spread out informally on the ground, with wild grape leaves for plates, she gave an exclamation of delight.

"Isn't it heavenly?" she cried.

Alec laughed. "I believe, Blue Bonnet, that your idea of heaven is to live in a wickiup and subsist on mustang grapes and wild berries indefinitely,—now isn't it?"

"Exactly—except that I'd add some of the bacon Knight is preparing to give us. That's the way the cowboys cook it."

Knight had cut a dozen or more twigs having a forked branch at the tip; on the end of each he placed a slice of bacon and then handed around the "forks" ceremoniously. "I'm not going to offer you anything so dainty as toasted moonshine," he explained, "but it's a heap more substantial."

They all gathered gypsy-fashion about the fire, toasting the bacon and their faces impartially; then transferring the crisp curly brown strips to the big slices of bread, devoured them with exclamations of approval that were most grateful to the arranger of the feast. Even canned cream failed to detract from the flavor of the coffee, and they consumed great quantities of the fragrant beverage, even Sarah partaking most intemperately.

Only a lot of ponies inured to the hardships of the round-up would have remained patient through the frolics of that day, and some of these wiry ponies looked rather drooping when the picnickers turned towards camp.

Mrs. Clyde, who had been watching the road rather anxiously as the shadows began to lengthen, brightened at once when Blue Bonnet's cheery call sounded through the trees.

"Oh, Grandmother, we've had the most gorgeous time in the world!" Blue Bonnet cried, as she flung herself out of the saddle. "Did you ever see such a beautifully mussed-up crowd in all your life?"

"If that is an evidence of a 'gorgeous time' you must certainly have had one," Mrs. Clyde smiled as her glance travelled from one rumpled and spotted We are Seven to another.

"These are the only skirts we brought and mine is all spluttered up with bacon," mourned Sarah.

"I think you will all have to go to bed while I wash them," the Senora suggested laughingly.

"Grandmother, please don't let Sarah play upon your sympathies. She doesn't appreciate how becoming a little dirt is to her peculiar style of beauty. She looks almost—human." The look of pained surprise Sarah turned on her sent Blue Bonnet off in a fit of merriment. "Oh, for a picture of that expression!" she cried. "And that reminds me,—I told all the boys to be at the Spring in fifteen minutes. There is plenty of light for a snap-shot and I've just a few films left."

"Oh, Blue Bonnet, haven't you done enough tramping to-day?" her grandmother exclaimed. "You ought to rest."

Blue Bonnet shook her head. "I can't rest till I get that picture. I want the boys and the We are Sevens on the little rustic bridge. Now, Sarah, don't you dare tidy up till I get you just as you are. I want you to pose as Terrible Tom the Texas Terror."

That Sarah had her own opinion as to who the Texas Terror might be was shown by her expression as she relinquished her design of brushing her hair, and followed the other girls up the hill to the Big Spring.

The boys were already assembled and were now grouped on the bridge in attitudes meant to be artistic and fetching.

The rustic bridge—rather more rustic than substantial—was suspended just over a pretty waterfall, which slipped down a smooth runway of eight or ten feet into a pool all foam and spray; a charming spot for a group-picture. It required both skill and patience to get every one posed and the camera focussed; Blue Bonnet had just completed these preliminaries, when Alec upset everything by insisting that he should be the photographer and she a member of the group. The rest supported his contention that she should be in the picture, and in the argument that followed, the chances for any picture at all grew slim.

Just then Uncle Joe appeared, and was at once pressed into service. Blue Bonnet gave explicit directions as to the precise moment at which the bulb was to be pressed, and then proceeded to join the rest who were in the agonies of trying to look pleasant.

"Do hurry, Blue Bonnet," urged Sarah nervously, "I can hear the bridge creaking."

A roar of derision followed this declaration and some of the smaller boys began stamping on the old timbers for the sheer joy of seeing poor Sarah quake. At the precise moment that Blue Bonnet stepped from the bank to her place by the rail, there was a loud report, followed by a scream.

Uncle Joe, looking up from the reflector, saw the bridge parted neatly in the middle, and the entire party shooting the chutes in a most informal manner. By the time the first boy had finished the descent, Uncle Joe was in the water fishing out the gasping victims. The pool was not deep, but the swift fall carried the smaller lads under the surface, and they came up too dazed to see the hands held out to seize them. Knight and Sandy found their feet at once, and with Uncle Joe formed a dam against which the others were caught like salmon in a river-trap.

Sarah was fished up by her blond braids and came up gasping, "I told you so!" before she opened her eyes.

"That's about as busy a spell as I've had for some time," Uncle Joe declared as he hauled out the last of the small boys and then clambered up the steep bank.

"You showed great presence of mind, Uncle Joe—except for one thing," said Blue Bonnet. "If you had just taken a snapshot when the bridge broke I'd be quite happy."

"And if a few of us had drowned while he was doing it—" Kitty began ironically.

"You'd have missed being in the picture, poor souls! Well, since we're all alive, let's go break the news gently to the grown-ups." Blue Bonnet looked around the drenched, shivering group and then burst into peals of laughter.

In truth they were a sorry looking lot. Soaked to the skin, with hair and clothes dripping and bedraggled, they all looked at each other as if surprised and grieved to find themselves part of so undignified a company.

Grandmother's expression when the We are Sevens hove into sight, sent Blue Bonnet off into another gale of merriment.

"We've been shooting the chutes, Grandmother," she said with dancing eyes.

"Without a boat," added Kitty.

It took Sarah to tell the story in all its harrowing details, and at its conclusion Mrs. Clyde looked sober.

"Were you really in danger?" she asked Blue Bonnet.

"Not a bit," Blue Bonnet declared. "Sarah was the only one who came near drowning and that was because she *would* talk under water."

Fifteen minutes later the little sheet-iron stove was red-hot, and on a hastily strung clothes-line about it hung an array of dripping garments that almost hid it from view.

"There's one comfort about all this," said Kitty, "our skirts and middies have had a much-needed bath."

"I'm afraid they won't be very clean,—cold water won't take grease out," said Sarah mournfully. "And I'd like to know— how are we going to iron them?"

They were all sitting in a circle about a blazing bonfire of Uncle Joe's building, with their streaming hair spread out to dry. Dressing-gowns and bedroom slippers had made it unnecessary to go to bed while their wardrobe hung on the line, and now that they were warm and comfortable, they were disposed to look on the adventure of the afternoon as more of a lark than a misfortune.

"Do you recall a prophecy you made this morning, Blue Bonnet?" asked Kitty.

Blue Bonnet shook her head.

"Your 'prophetic soul' told you, if I remember rightly, that we were going to conduct ourselves like a model Sunday-school class to-day."

"Well, if anybody would promise me as much fun in Sunday-school as I've had this day, I'd never be absent or tardy!"

laughed Blue Bonnet.

Sarah looked pained. "It's Sunday to-morrow," she remarked. "I wonder what Dr. Judson will take as the text of his sermon."

Blue Bonnet gave her a long, curious glance. "Do you really wonder, Sarah, about things like that?"

Sarah raised honest, serious eyes. "Why, of course, Blue Bonnet. Don't you?"

"No," she confessed, "but I do wonder—at you!"

As they sat silent for a moment about the blazing logs, Blue Bonnet had an inspiration.

"Grandmother," she asked abruptly, "are you very hungry?"

"Why—is it your turn to get dinner?" Mrs. Clyde smiled; she was shaking the water from her granddaughter's long hair, and spreading it in the warm rays of the fire.

"No, Amanda and I were to get lunch. But are you?"

"Not at all. Mrs. Judson and I had an excellent dinner at noon."

"Well, I've a splendid idea. There are heaps of hot ashes down under the logs. We can bury some potatoes there,—the cowboys cook them that way and they are delicious. Then with some devilled-ham sandwiches we could sit right here and eat, and have no tiresome dishes to wash up afterwards."

"Hear, hear!" cried Kitty and Debby.

"It's easy to see whose turn it is to wash dishes," laughed Amanda.

"It's right handsome of you, Blue Bonnet," Kitty remarked gratefully, "—especially when it wasn't your turn to officiate. I'll make the sandwiches and Debby—you get the potatoes."

That buffet supper was later pronounced the most successful meal ever prepared in *Poco Tiempo*.

"This is truly Bohemian," remarked Mrs. Clyde, as with a newspaper for both plate and napkin, she joined the group about the fire, "—much more so than the studio-luncheons they call Bohemian in Boston."

"Fancy anything trying to be Bohemian in Boston!" exclaimed Blue Bonnet. "They haven't a thing in common."

"They both begin with a B," said Sarah.

The girls were too surprised to laugh.

"Is that a joke, Sarah?" asked Kitty in an awestruck tone.

"Of course not,—they do, don't they?" she returned.

As the girls collapsed at this, she looked up in puzzled surprise. "I'd like to know what's so funny about that," she remarked plaintively.

"There comes Mrs. Judson," exclaimed Debby.

There was a hasty wiping of blackened fingers on newspaper napkins as the girls rose to greet this unexpected guest. The little figure approaching them seemed slighter than ever, and the gingham dress fairly trailed over the long grass. The face was hidden in the inevitable sunbonnet.

"Hello, everybody, are you dry yet?" called a cheerful voice.

"Carita!" exclaimed Blue Bonnet. "We thought you were your mother."

Carita looked down at her loosely fitting garment and laughed. "I had to wear this while my dress dried. Knight said I ought to hang out a sign—'room to let.' Mother made me wear the sunbonnet because my hair is still wet. But I said I could dry it by your fire as well as anywhere else." She tossed away the cavernous bonnet and the chestnut locks fell in a cloud about her shoulders. With her dark eyes and skin framed by the long straight hair she looked like a young Indian.

"Have a potato?" asked Blue Bonnet, spearing one with a stick and presenting it to the guest.

"Thank you." Carita took it as if this were the usual fashion of serving this vegetable, and ate it with the ease born of long experience. Suddenly she gave an exclamation. "Oh, I nearly forgot. Alec sent over something. The boys couldn't come for they've nothing to wear but blankets—they're rolled up like a lot of mummies around the fire. But Alec and Knight and Sandy have been writing something,—I think it's a letter."

"It's a poem!—oh, Blue Bonnet, you read it aloud." Kitty handed over the verses and in the flickering light they gathered close about Blue Bonnet as she read:

THE BRIDGE

"We stood on a bridge in Texas,

Near a camp far, far from town;
We stood there in broad daylight,—
'Cause there wasn't room to sit down.

"We posed on that bridge so rustic,
To be snapped by Uncle Joe,
And we smiled and looked real pleasant,
Yet one heart was filled with woe.

"For a stream, both swift and deadly,
Flowed beneath the bridgelet there,
And the creaking of the timbers
Gave this timid maid a scare.

"As sweeping eddying 'neath us
The deep, dark waters rolled,
She could seem to see our finish—
Dashed beneath the waters cold.

"Yet the bridge still held, but trembled,
—Gleamed the torrent chilly, vast,—
And the weight of one Blue Bonnet
Broke the camel's back at last!"

"Who did it?" cried Blue Bonnet.

"All three helped," said Carita. "But I think Sandy did most."

"He must be cleverer than he looks," said Blue Bonnet.

"Why, don't you think he looks clever?" exclaimed Kitty, "I do."

"It wasn't clever of him to have sandy hair," Blue Bonnet declared perversely.

"As if he could help it!" said Sarah.

"We must write a 'pome,' too," said Blue Bonnet.

"We?" exclaimed Debby. "I never found two words to rhyme in all my life. You and Kitty are the only ones who ever 'drop into poetry.'"

"The muse must be partial to red hair," said Amanda. And though Kitty sniffed insultedly at this insinuation, her bright head was soon bent over a pad beside Blue Bonnet's, and after much chewing of their pencils and shrieks of laughter at impossible rhymes, the two of them finally evolved the following:

WE ARE SEVEN

"You marvel that a simple band
Of maidens, young and fair,
Should linger ever on the land,
Nor for the water care?

"If you should ask in dulcet tone
Why for the earth they sigh,
They'll weep, they'll shriek, they'll give a groan,—
But they will answer why.

"'Last night we were a happy bunch,
Last night about eleven—'
Quoth you—'But why this sorry lot?
How many members have you got?'
They'll answer—'We Are Seven.'

"'But seven are not all alive?'
'Yea, yea, thou trifling varlet,
Though here we number only five,—

Two caught a fever scarlet."

"'And o'er us five whose courage great
Brought us to far-off Texas,
There seems to brood an awful fate,
And trials sore to vex us."

"'To-day the bridge on which we stood
And posed above the rippling wave,
Alas! was made of rotten wood
And plunged us in a watery grave.'"

"'Then ye are dead! All five are dead!
Their spirits are in heaven!'
'Tis throwing words away, for still
These maidens five will have their will,
And answer—'We Are Seven!'"

"I wonder what Mr. Wordsworth would say to that?" said Debby, when this effort had been heard and elaborately praised.

"He's dead," remarked Sarah. Then, ignoring Debby's snicker she continued: "It's very good, Blue Bonnet,—but you shouldn't have said that two had the scarlet fever. There's only one, really."

"Poetic license!" Kitty claimed fiercely.

"I think you are the cleverest girls I ever heard of!" Carita exclaimed. "I'm going to run right over with that poem—I can't wait for the boys to see it."

Snatching up her bonnet Carita ran back to the other camp; while the girls, quite tired out by the excitement and varied adventures of the day, prepared to go to bed. As they neared the tents there came a familiar sound from the direction of Camp Judson. It was the loud jangle of cowbells.

"Do you suppose those boys are going to eat at this time of night?" asked Sarah.

"Of course not, Sallykins," said Debby. "Don't you understand?—that's the boys applauding our poets!"

C. E. Jacobs & Edyth Ellerbeck Read

CHAPTER XV

SUNDAY

"FOR once in my life," said Blue Bonnet, with a long-drawn sigh, "I'm ready for a day of rest."

"Please don't begin to rest till you've done the dishes," begged Kitty.

Blue Bonnet tossed her head scornfully. "I wouldn't trouble trouble till trouble troubles you, Kitty-Kat. If you can go to church with as clear a conscience as mine, I'll take off my hat to you. One lapse doesn't make a sinner!"

"One?" Kitty echoed, and would have continued scathingly had not Sarah interrupted with—

"I don't see how we can go to church with such looking clothes."

"Sarah's regretting the white pique skirt you wouldn't let her bring," said Kitty.

"Why, Sarah," Blue Bonnet turned a pained look on the serious young person, "I would never have believed you would be one to stay away from church for lack of an Easter bonnet."

"I didn't mention Easter—nor bonnets either," Sarah declared indignantly. "The idea,—to hear you girls talk any one would think I was completely wrapped up in clothes!"

"Everybody is, you know—except savages," returned Blue Bonnet.

Sarah's expression at this caused Mrs. Clyde to rise hurriedly and vanish within her tent. Freed from this restraint Kitty went on wickedly:

"Anyway, Dr. Judson has been a missionary in Africa and I'm sure he'd excuse you if—"

Sarah left the table with great dignity, leaving the other girls weak with laughter.

Carita appeared a little later with her denim dress looking fresh, clean, and wrinkleless.

"It looks as if it had just been ironed," Sarah silently commented. When Mrs. Clyde called to the girls that it was time to go over to Camp Judson, Miss Blake was nowhere to be found.

The church service was held in the "Druid's Grove," a place of mingled shade and sunshine, where a little tumbling creek was the only accompaniment to the hymns, and the birds trilled an obligato. An old tree-stump served as pulpit, and here Dr. Judson talked rather than preached to his youthful congregation.

Blue Bonnet, listening to him, unconsciously let her eyes wander, as they always did in the church at Woodford, in search of the memorial window 'Sacred to the memory of Elizabeth Clyde Ashe' that was inseparably linked in her mind with religious service. Instead of the figure of the Good Shepherd with the lamb in his arms, the branches of the live oaks here formed a Gothic arch, in the shadow of which sat Mrs. Judson with little Joe asleep on her lap. The look on the mother's face was full of the same brooding tenderness that the artist had given to the eyes of the Shepherd of Old.

When they rose to sing, the young voices rang out clear and joyous, quite unlike the droning that too often passes for singing in a grown-up congregation.

"Bright youth and snow-crowned age,
Strong men and maidens meek:
Raise high your free, exulting song!
God's wondrous praises speak!

"With all the angel choirs,
With all the saints of earth,
Pour out the strains of joy and bliss,
True rapture, noblest mirth!"

The stirring verses, sung with a will by every one, seemed to soar to the very tree-tops, making the branches sway with the rhythm and spirit of the hymn.

Blue Bonnet heaved a sigh of regret as they rose to leave the grove. "It's so sweet,—I wish it could last all day."

"I don't remember ever having heard you make a remark like that about church before," remarked Kitty.

"I don't care much for anything that's held indoors," Blue Bonnet confessed. "And I don't like preachers who make their voices sound like the long-stop on an organ. Now that last hymn we sang makes me fairly bubble inside."

"Don't let Sarah hear you say that. She seems to think one ought to draw a long face on the Sabbath,—a sort of 'world-without-end' expression, you know. I believe she thinks it almost wicked to be happy on Sunday."

"Well, Sarah may be as blue as she likes,—this is the kind of a day that makes me feel bright pink!"

"Where is Sarah, anyway?" asked Kitty. "I haven't seen her since breakfast. Surely she didn't miss the service?"

"No, I saw her sitting by a big tree 'way at the back," said Amanda.

"It isn't like Sarah to take a back seat—at church," remarked Blue Bonnet. "I believe she must be cross because we teased her this morning."

Grandmother and Sarah were already deep in preparations for dinner when the others straggled into camp. The well-cooked meal of muffins, fried ham, potatoes and stewed dried fruit they served met with visible as well as audible approval.

"Picnic lunches are more fun, but this kind of a meal is more—filling," said Blue Bonnet. "Let's eat all we can now and have just bread and milk for supper—we've two cans of fresh milk in the creek."

"Blue Bonnet seems to have developed a sudden liking for 'jarring notes,' doesn't she, girls?" asked Kitty.

When dinner was done and the dishes washed, they all sought the buck-board seats in the lounging room.

"If we only had a book now, it would be fine to have

Grandmother read aloud," remarked Blue Bonnet.

"You wouldn't let Sarah bring any books," Amanda reminded her.

"Nevertheless, methinks Sarah looks as if she had one up her sleeve," said Debby.

"Not up my sleeve," Sarah confessed, "—but in my bag. I'll go get it,—it's 'Don Quixote,' in Spanish and English both."

"Did you bring the drawn-work, too?" asked Kitty. "My, Sarah, but you are a first-rate smuggler!"

"Now that suspicion has raised its snaky head, I'd like to know—why is Sarah, long after the dishes are done, still wearing that apron?" Blue Bonnet had sent a random shot, but to her surprise Sarah flushed to the roots of her blond hair.

She rose hastily to go in search of "Don Quixote," but the other girls were too quick for her. They pitilessly tore the shielding apron from her shoulders, and the newly sponged and pressed middy jacket and khaki skirt stood revealed in all their guilty freshness.

"They've been ironed!" gasped Kitty.

"What do you think of that for selfishness,—not to let a soul know she had an iron?" demanded Debby.

"I got it over at Mrs. Judson's. And none of you said you wanted an iron," said Sarah.

"And do you mean to say that our Sarah, daughter of the Reverend Samuel Blake, wilfully broke the Sabbath by ironing?" Concentrated horror appeared on Kitty's saucy countenance.

"She probably thinks 'the better the day the better the deed,'" said Blue Bonnet.

"If Mrs. Judson could press Carita's dress, I don't see that it was any worse for me to press mine," Sarah protested. "I'm used to looking respectable at church."

"It's no wonder you refused to sit by so unrespectable a crowd as the rest of us!" exclaimed Blue Bonnet.

Mrs. Clyde was laughing inwardly, but she came to the aid of the unhappy Sarah.

"I think good nature has ceased to be a virtue, Sarah," she declared. "Hereafter you have my permission to resort to violence if necessary to protect yourself. Quiet down, girls,—remember it is Sunday."

Much relieved, Sarah brought forth the contraband book and the long peaceful afternoon was spent in listening to the various mishaps that befell the valiant Don and his faithful Sancho Panza.

"If it weren't for setting a dangerous precedent, I'd tell Sarah how glad we all are that she defied the authorities and did some smuggling," remarked Kitty. She and Debby had gone to the creek to bring up the milk for supper, and now made a pretty picture as they came up the willow-grown path, bearing the tall cans.

"You look like somebody-or-other at the well," Blue Bonnet declared as Kitty came into sight.

C. E. Jacobs & Edyth Ellerbeck Read

"Are you sure you don't mean thing-a-ma-bob?" laughed Kitty. "If you mean Rebecca, I don't agree with you. I'll wager Rebecca never wore a middy blouse or carried a tin milk-can!"

That evening the inmates of both camps again sat about a big bonfire. But this time the frolics and rollicking airs had given way to a decorous singing of patriotic songs, stirring hymns and a pleasant "sermonette" by the pastor of this youthful flock.

Long after this Sunday was past, Blue Bonnet remembered it as one of the sweetest Sabbaths she had ever spent; and she could never decide just what part of the day she had liked most,—the hour in the Druid's Grove; the afternoon when Grandmother with her pleasant voice had read aloud from "Don Quixote;" or the evening, when they sat about the glowing logs, alternately singing, and listening to Dr. Judson.

"I'm going to ask Sandy to recite," Knight whispered to her as there fell a silence.

"Get him to do 'The Bridge!'" Blue Bonnet said with dancing eyes.

"I'm sure he'd rather do 'We are Seven,'" he replied, laughing.

"I wish he'd recite the 'Hymn of the Alamo,'" said Alec, who had overheard the conversation. "Ask him to, Knight,—he'll do anything for you, and that's a fine poem."

"Alec wrote an essay on the Alamo," Blue Bonnet explained to Knight, "and it won a prize—the Sargent prize—in our school this year."

Alec squirmed with a boyish dislike of hearing himself praised; but Knight slapped him on the shoulder enthusiastically.

"Bully for you, old chap! Tell the fellows the story of the Alamo, will you? Uncle Bayard likes them to hear historical things like that—can't hear them too often."

Alec looked horrified at the idea, but Blue Bonnet joined Knight in urging him. "You tell the story of the fight and maybe Sandy will finish with the Hymn."

Sandy promising to do his part, Alec finally yielded. Sinking far back in the shadow where his face could not be seen by any of the great circle of listeners, and his voice came out of the blackness with a decided tremor in it, the boy told, and told well, the story of the frontier riflemen in their struggle for the liberation of Texas from the yoke of the Mexican dictator.

How the Texas lads thrilled at the recital of heroism, and thrilled at the mention of such names as Travis and Crockett! It was not a new tale; not a boy there but knew the story of that handful of men—less than two hundred of them—who, barricading themselves within the Alamo fortress, for ten days defied the Mexicans, over four thousand strong; only to be massacred to a man in the final heartrending fall.

Alec's voice lost its tremor and ended with a patriotic ring that made Blue Bonnet glow with pride—pride in the heroes he told of, and in the friend who told of them.

"It just needs Colonel Potter's poem to add the right climax to that bit of history," Dr. Judson declared; and Sandy stood up at once.

C. E. Jacobs & Edyth Ellerbeck Read

Sandy was used to "talking on his feet;" and he stood in an easy posture, tossing his light reddish hair back from his broad forehead, and with one hand resting lightly on the alpenstock he had been carving for Blue Bonnet.

Listening to him, Blue Bonnet lost all her early prejudice against the clever lad, and responding to the unbounded enthusiasm and the true orator's ring in the boyish voice, thrilled warmly to the spirit of the lines:

HYMN OF THE ALAMO

"Arise! Man the wall—our clarion blast
Now sounds its final reveille,—
This dawning morn must be the last
Our fated band shall ever see.
To life, but not to hope, farewell;
Yon trumpet's clang and cannon's peal,
And storming shout and clash of steel
Is *ours*,—but not our country's knell.
Welcome the Spartan's death!
'Tis no despairing strife—
We fall, we die—but our expiring breath
Is freedom's breath of life!

"Here, on this new Thermopylae,
Our monument shall tower on high,
And 'Alamo' hereafter be
On bloodier fields the battle-cry!"
Thus Travis from the rampart cried;
And when his warriors saw the foe
Like whelming billows surge below,—
At once each dauntless heart replied:
"Welcome the Spartan's death!
'Tis no despairing strife—
We fall—but our expiring breath

Is freedom's breath of life!"

As Sandy resumed his seat amid a hush that was a greater tribute than applause, Blue Bonnet turned to Knight with glowing eyes.

"And to think those brave fellows did all that for Texas! Aren't you proud to belong to this state?"

"You'd better believe I am!"

"We've had some heroes in Massachusetts," Alec reminded them.

"And they were all *Americans*—and so are we." Knight's bigger way of looking at the matter settled what threatened to grow into an argument.

"That Sandy boy's a wonder," Blue Bonnet exclaimed. "I take back every uncomplimentary remark I ever made about him. Appearances are so deceiving."

"'All that glitters isn't gold,'" said Knight, looking like his uncle as he gravely quoted this ancient maxim.

"It's a pity it isn't,—Sandy would be a millionaire with that hair of his!" Blue Bonnet laughed.

"I mean 'handsome is as handsome does,'" said Knight, "—that isn't quite so dangerous a quotation. I expect to see Sandy President some day, or at least a senator."

"Can't you imagine the newspaper headings: 'Senator Red-top of Texas'—?" laughed Blue Bonnet.

"He's hoping to go East to college this fall," Knight remarked more seriously.

"It's queer," said Alec, "how all the Western boys long to go East and all the Eastern fellows think they're just made if they can come West. I'd like to trade him my chance at Harvard for his health and strength."

"Can't you arrange that trifling exchange for Alec?" Blue Bonnet asked Knight.

He shook his head. "Sandy won't take anybody's chances,— he's the sort that makes his own."

"Some of us aren't allowed to."

Alec's voice had suddenly grown moody, and Blue Bonnet thought it time to change the subject. In a moment her clear, sweet voice was leading the rest in "The Flag without a Stain."

"How do you like a Texas Sunday?" Blue Bonnet found herself beside Sarah as they walked back to *Poco Tiempo*, and put the question rather mischievously.

"It's been very nice, most of it," Sarah returned in a stiff manner, very unlike her usual one.

"What part didn't you like?"

Sarah made sure that the others were not listening, then answered in a tone Blue Bonnet had never heard from her before:

"I didn't like being made to feel that whatever I do is the wrong thing. I never seem to please you any more, Blue Bonnet."

"Why, Sarah!" Blue Bonnet stopped still and gazed at Sarah in consternation. Sarah paused, too, and in the faint rays from the fire the two girls looked at each other steadily for a moment without speaking. Finally Blue Bonnet blurted out:

"I wish you'd tell me just what you mean."

"I mean that I've come to the conclusion that I should have stayed in Woodford. I don't seem to fit in here." Sarah's voice shook a little.

"Sarah!" was still all Blue Bonnet could stammer. It was all so sudden and unexpected; a bolt from a clear sky.

"Please don't think I'm thin-skinned and can't stand a little teasing," Sarah continued, "for I'm sure I can—I always have had to. But lately I haven't said a thing that hasn't made one or other of you 'hoot' as Kitty says. And everything I've wanted to do you've thought ridiculous. Lately the boys have begun to laugh at me; even those I hardly know."

This time Blue Bonnet said nothing; she was overcome by the thought that all Sarah had said was quite true. She hastily reviewed the past few weeks, and as one by one she remembered various incidents, the force of Sarah's complaints struck her anew.

Kitty's dare and that wild ride; the ban put upon Sarah's Spanish books and the much-loved drawn-work; and, lately, the almost concerted effort of all of them to convert everything Sarah said and did into something unwarranted and absurd. By the time Blue Bonnet had reached her own action of that very morning in tearing the apron forcibly from Sarah's shoulders, she was dumb with shame. This was the way she had rewarded her friend for a loyalty that had been unswerving through all that dreadful week in

Woodford, when the other girls had sent her to Coventry; for all her sweet thoughtfulness that had proved itself unfailing!

She suddenly threw her arms impulsively around Sarah's shoulders and faced her squarely.

"I've been downright horrid," she said earnestly. "And a rude, selfish hostess. I haven't any right to expect you to forgive me, Sarah, dear, but if you can find it in your heart to give another chance, I'll show you I can and will be different."

"It isn't serious enough to talk of forgiveness," Sarah said in her honest, straightforward way. "All I want to know is, that you're not—sorry—I came."

"Sarah, don't say that! You make me hate myself!" Blue Bonnet shook her almost fiercely. "You mustn't think it either. I'm glad, glad, glad you came! I've meant you to know it, and I've wanted you to have a splendid time, and here all the while—" she stopped and swallowed hard.

Sarah's face lighted up happily and she did what was for her an unprecedented thing,—she drew Blue Bonnet to her and gave her a hearty hug.

"That's all I wanted to know," she said. "Please don't imagine I haven't enjoyed myself, Blue Bonnet. It's been the most wonderful visit! I'm queer, I know, but I can't help liking the things I like, and if only the girls would stop trying to make me over—"

"I'll make them!" Blue Bonnet declared; and at this threat they both laughed, and the storm was over.

CHAPTER XVI

THE LOST SHEEP

"OH, Carita, do you really have to go to-day?" Genuine regret was in Blue Bonnet's eyes and tone.

Carita sighed.

"Yes, Grandfather expects us back at the farm to-night, and Mother never disappoints him. He's getting old and she doesn't like to leave him alone much. We may come up again before the summer is over,—Father has to be here for several weeks yet."

"But we'll be gone,—we're to leave on Wednesday, you know. Did ever days fly so before? I haven't seen half enough of you, Carita."

"You seem to belong to so many people," Carita said rather wistfully, "I've been afraid to claim too much of your time. But there are other summers. Maybe when you come back from the East next year you can come to the farm,—it isn't much of a journey on the cars."

Blue Bonnet lost herself a moment in reflection. "When she came back from the East"—why, she hadn't even decided

C. E. Jacobs & Edyth Ellerbeck Read

that she was going East again—yet.

"And you can come to see me—at the Blue Bonnet ranch," she said.

Carita shook her head.

"Railroad fares are pretty high. We have to be very careful since Father lost his health. That's why we came back from India, you know. The doctors said that this climate was best for his trouble, and when Grandfather offered us a home on the farm we were so glad. But Father's not having a church—only once in a while when he fills a pulpit for a few weeks at a time—keeps us a little short. I reckon you don't know much about—being short. You have everything you want, don't you?"

"Everybody seems to think that; they forget that I haven't a mother or father—or any brothers and sisters," Blue Bonnet said very simply.

Carita threw her arms impulsively about her friend and gave her a warm kiss. "How mean of me to forget! I wish you were my sister. Boys don't always understand. But you have so many people to love you, you can't ever get lonesome. And having lots of money must be so nice, and to go away to school, and have pretty clothes and go to parties and travel, why—" Carita's breath failed her.

"I ought to be mighty thankful. And I am most of the time," Blue Bonnet replied. "But the people who love you always expect a great deal of you, and it's very hard to live up to their expectations. Besides, going to school isn't all fun, I can tell you."

"I wouldn't care if it weren't all fun, if I could only go. Father teaches me at home, but we have so many interruptions. There are dishes to wash, babies to mind, Grandfather to wait upon, till neither of us knows whether we're doing arithmetic or grammar." Carita rose. "I must hurry back to camp—Mother's packing."

"You never forget what's expected of you, do you?" Blue Bonnet asked, with a mixture of wonder and admiration.

"It wouldn't do for me to forget,—I'm the eldest, you know. Mother depends on me." Carita spoke as though it were the most natural thing in the world for a fourteen-year-old girl to be "depended upon."

"Nobody ever depends on me—for a very good reason!" Blue Bonnet laughed. "Somehow it's so much easier for me to forget than to remember. It's the only thing I do with shining success."

"You'll learn to be responsible when you have children of your own," Carita said as sagely as if she were forty instead of fourteen.

Blue Bonnet's eyes shone.

"I'm going to have a whole dozen!" she declared.

"I wouldn't, if I were you—it would be so hard on the eldest," Carita reminded her.

And Blue Bonnet, noticing the care-worn look in the eyes of her "missionary girl," decided that being the eldest of a big family might have its disadvantages.

"Grandmother, I wish there were something I could do for Carita," she said later that morning, as she and Mrs. Clyde found themselves alone.

"You have already done a great deal for her," her grand-mother remarked. "Mrs. Judson has told me how much your letters and presents have meant to Carita."

"But that was so little,—and it was just fun for me. She has all work and no play, and I don't think it's fair."

"Perhaps you can do something for her, later on. But you must be careful how you assume responsibilities, Blue Bonnet. You seem to have taken upon yourself a great many already."

"What ones?" Blue Bonnet questioned in surprise.

"In the first place—you've me!" Grandmother smiled.

"That's so,—I'm responsible to Aunt Lucinda for you. And what others?"

"How about the We are Sevens whom you've brought so far away from their homes? And Alec?"

Blue Bonnet's eyes opened.

"I hadn't thought of them in that way. But I reckon you're right. And there's Solomon, too."

Grandmother's mouth twitched. "You must be sure you can do your full duty by the responsibilities you have before you assume new ones."

Blue Bonnet looked very serious. "Seems to me life has a heap of complications. Now there's Alec,—he's worse than a complication. He's a downright puzzle."

"Has he said anything more about his trouble?" Mrs. Clyde asked.

"Just hints. But they sound as if he were hiding something pretty bad. Sometimes I wish he would come right out with it, and then again, I'm afraid. If he keeps on looking dark and broody every time the conversation turns on the subject of health, I'm going to write the General about it. I think *that's* my duty."

"But Alec looks wonderfully well, bigger, broader and better in every way than when he left Woodford," Mrs. Clyde insisted.

"I know he does. But when I remarked to Knight how well Alec looked, and said I thought he ought to get rid of his foolish notion about himself now, Knight looked queer and asked, 'Do you think it a foolish notion? I think he's dead right.' And Knight's a sensible boy and wouldn't say that unless he thought so."

Mrs. Clyde's eyes reflected Blue Bonnet's look of perplexity. "Have you talked with your uncle about him?"

"No. Just after I talked with you Alec asked me not to mention the matter to any one else. That shuts out Uncle Cliff. I'm sorry, for I'm sure he'd suggest the right thing. There comes Miguel with the horses. You don't mind our riding a little way with the Judsons do you? They're nearly ready to start."

"No, so long as you are back for lunch," said her grandmother.

The boys had all gone hunting early that morning, and only the girls of *Poco Tiempo* were on hand to escort the departing guests. Mrs. Clyde said good-bye to Mrs. Judson with genuine regret, and kissed all the small Judsons warmly at parting.

The whole family was packed into the two seats of the heavy farm-wagon, the mother driving with one of the boys beside her; Carita in the back seat holding Joe and, at the same time, keeping a watchful eye on the two lively youngsters by her side. Bedding and camp equipment were heaped high in the wagon-box.

"You look like a picture of 'Crossing the Plains,'" Blue Bonnet exclaimed.

"Play you're the Injuns going to scalp us!" begged Carita's brother Harry, his big dark eyes shining with eagerness.

Blue Bonnet gave a shrill "Ho, ye ho, ho!" that passed for a war-whoop, and in a minute they were all off, the farm horses rather startled at the carryings-on; the small boys wild with excitement; and the We are Sevens tearing madly down the road "ki-yi-ing" at the top of their voices.

Mrs. Clyde turned with a smile to Dr. Judson, who stood looking rather amazedly after his departing family. "Blue Bonnet is alternately five and fifteen," she remarked.

"She is decidedly refreshing," he returned. "I hope you will try to keep her a child as long as possible."

"I don't need to try!" she replied with a laugh.

The parting between the "emigrants" and the Indians was not such as history records of leave-takings between these sworn enemies. Carita had to wink hard to keep back the tears when she said good-bye to Blue Bonnet, and the little Judsons set up a loud wail when their former pursuers waved them farewell.

"It's a shame Carita has to go back and slave on that old farm," Blue Bonnet declared, as she looked after the little figure holding on to the baby with one hand and waving her handkerchief in the other.

"It seems selfish of us to be having a whole summer of fun when she's only had two or three days," said Sarah.

"Sarah talks as if it's downright wicked for any of us to be having a good time," Kitty retorted. "Maybe you think one of us ought to change places with Carita?" she challenged Sarah.

"Sarah is the only one of us that's unselfish enough to do such a thing!" Blue Bonnet exclaimed warmly; and Sarah sent her a grateful glance.

They were in a part of the country that Blue Bonnet called "the other side of the hills,"—a land of sheep-ranches, for the most part; rather barren and level, unlike the rolling green prairie of the cattle-country she loved. They could see the Judson's wagon winding its way across the plain, until only a blur of dust marked its course towards the horizon.

"Let's hurry," said Blue Bonnet, "I promised Grandmother we'd surely be back for lunch."

"It isn't your turn to cook, is it?" asked Kitty.

"No,—it's my turn to eat!" And Blue Bonnet, urging Firefly, was off at a lively clip towards camp.

"Please stop, Blue Bonnet," panted Kitty after a few minutes of this sort of going. "I've a dreadful pain in my side."

Blue Bonnet good-naturedly fell back with her, and the rest swept past them with a chorus of taunts for being "quitters." Both girls looked after Comanche and his rider with something like wonder in their eyes. Sarah was riding like a veteran; it was plain that she and Comanche understood each other at last.

"Sarah's coming on, isn't she?" said Kitty.

"Coming?—I think she's arrived!" Blue Bonnet exclaimed.

"She can thank me for picking out Comanche for her," remarked Kitty; she preferred herself to be the object of Blue Bonnet's approbation and could not be roused to much enthusiasm on Sarah's account.

"Considering your motive, Kitty-Kat, I'm not so sure Sarah owes you any gratitude," laughed Blue Bonnet. Suddenly she gave an exclamation. "Why, there's a lamb,—I wonder if it's dead."

"Where?" asked Kitty.

Blue Bonnet pointed to a spot some distance off the road, but Kitty's city-bred eyes could make out nothing. Just then there came a feeble bleat, and in a second Blue Bonnet had slipped from the saddle and handed the reins to Kitty.

"Hold Firefly a minute, please. That *is* a lamb!"

Kitty obediently held the unwilling Firefly, while Blue Bonnet hurried in the direction of the bleat. A moment later she stooped, and when she straightened up, there was a small woolly object in her arms.

"It's too little to travel and the mean old mother's gone off with the flock," Blue Bonnet said, coming up with the deserted baby.

"What are you going to do with it?" demanded Kitty helplessly.

"I'm going to find the flock. It's been driven along here and inside that fence. I'm going to let down the bars and cross the field. You see the little shanty over there?—I believe there must be a shepherd somewhere about, and I'll give him the lamb. He isn't a very good shepherd or he'd have been looking out for poor little lambs. Shady used to herd sheep and he's told me lots about it."

"And what shall I do?" asked Kitty. "I'm afraid to hold Firefly,—he nearly pulls me off the saddle."

"Then tie both horses to the bars here and help me with the lamb."

Kitty offered no protest. This was so like Blue Bonnet. It was always a stray dog or a lost baby, or an old woman at the poor-house that enlisted her ready sympathy; Kitty ran over a long list in her mind. Of course it had to be a lost lamb or a calf in Texas; the wonder was there hadn't been more of them.

Hastily tying both ponies to a fence-post with a scrambling knot of the reins that would have brought down Blue Bonnet's wrath upon her hapless head, Kitty hastened across the close-cropped meadow. It seemed to her they trudged miles, taking turns carrying the lamb, before they reached the little shack. A stupid young fellow, half-asleep, lay sprawled in the shade.

"Here's a lamb we found by the road," said Blue Bonnet, proffering her woolly burden.

Without uttering a word the sleepy youth took the lamb from her; but Blue Bonnet, observing his manner of handling it, saw that he was wise in the ways of sheep, and she was content to leave her charge with him.

"Flock's over there," he said at length, pointing vaguely with his thumb.

"All right. Come on, Kitty." As they turned away she said in an undertone: "Shady says the herders are alone so much they almost forget how to talk."

"He's evidently forgotten how to say 'thank you,'" Kitty said crossly. "Why, Blue Bonnet—where are the horses?"

"You ought to know. Where did you tie them?"

Kitty's startled eyes rested on the post beside the bars. "To that post there. Oh, Blue Bonnet, some one must have stolen them!"

"Stolen? Who'd steal them, I'd like to know? This comes, Kitty Clark, of letting you hitch a horse!" Blue Bonnet was straining her eyes for a sight of the runaways.

"This comes, Blue Bonnet Ashe, of following you on every wild-goose chase you choose to lead me!" Cross, tired and out of patience, Kitty flared up in one of her sudden outbursts, and Blue Bonnet took fire at once.

"If you think I'm going to let a poor creature starve to death rather than disturb your comfort, you're much mistaken!" An angry glance passed between them.

Sarah, the pacifier, was several miles away by this time; and even she would have felt her resources sorely taxed to meet this emergency. Miles from camp and no horses!

Kitty stalked into the road and started to walk, holding her head high and swinging her arms as though *she* didn't mind a little matter of five or six miles. Blue Bonnet, with the training of a lifetime, stopped to put up the bars before setting out on the long tramp. It was already noon and the sun glared down, unbearably hot. Before she had gone a mile Blue Bonnet looked about for a mesquite bush, and finding one sank down in its shade. Kitty kept doggedly on.

"Oh, Kitty!" Blue Bonnet called after her. "I've heard of people who hadn't sense enough to come in out of the rain, and I think it's a heap sillier not to have sense enough to come in out of the sun!"

Kitty wavered; and was lost. Turning back she threw herself beside Blue Bonnet with a groan.

"My feet are one big blister," she moaned, her anger swallowed up in the anguish of the moment.

"We can't possibly walk," said Blue Bonnet. "And I've an idea. If that cloud of dust I saw on the road towards camp was Firefly and Rowdy—and it probably was—the girls will soon be after us."

And so it proved; except that it was Alec and Knight instead of the girls who came riding furiously down the road in search of them. When Alec heard Blue Bonnet's ranch-call he threw his hat in the air with a whoop of relief.

"We've been looking for your mangled remains all along the way," he declared, as they reached the girls. "We had the

C. E. Jacobs & Edyth Ellerbeck Read

fright of our lives when Firefly and Rowdy came trotting into camp minus their riders."

"You thought we'd been thrown?" Blue Bonnet asked.

"I would have thought so if there had been only one, but it didn't seem likely that both of you could have come a cropper," Knight replied.

"Is Grandmother worried?" Blue Bonnet asked hastily.

"She doesn't know. The girls didn't tell her anything except that you and Kitty had loafed along the way. She didn't see the horses. But we'd better hurry back."

Each boy had led one of the errant ponies, and now the girls mounted and lost no time in getting back to camp.

"I'm so sorry—" Blue Bonnet began to speak as soon as she came within sight of her grandmother, "—I didn't mean to be so late."

"I can't quite understand, Blue Bonnet, why you and Kitty could not come back with the other girls. It is long past noon." Mrs. Clyde had been worried, and required more of an explanation than an apology. Blue Bonnet's tired face and dusty, dishevelled clothes spoke eloquently of adventure.

"I stopped to pick up a lamb,—its mother had gone on with the flock and left it to starve. Shady says lots of sheep don't care about their children. That's why he likes beef-critters best,—cows always make good mothers. And Kitty and I found the shepherd and gave him the lamb to take care of."

The annoyance faded from Grandmother's face and her eyes softened.

Uncle Joe, who had been an interested listener, spoke up— "Say, Honey, why didn't you bring the lamb home?—fresh meat is just what we've been needing."

"Uncle Joe!" Horror rang in Blue Bonnet's voice. "Do you think I'd have eaten that poor little darling?"

He scratched a puzzled head. "Why seems like I've known you to eat nice young roast lamb, Blue Bonnet."

"That's different," she insisted.

"The only acquaintances Blue Bonnet is willing to have roasted are her friends!" said Kitty; and Blue Bonnet generously let her have the last word.

C. E. Jacobs & Edyth Ellerbeck Read

CHAPTER XVII

SECRETS

"THERE'S only one thing nicer than going camping," Blue Bonnet declared.

Her grandmother looked up. "And that is—?"

"Getting home again!" Blue Bonnet laughed happily.

They were in sight of the ranch-house now, and could see the girls and Alec dismounting at the veranda steps. Don and Solomon leaping excitedly about the group, suddenly caught sight of the approaching buckboard and raced madly to meet their mistress. Even the horses seemed glad to be home again and tired as they were with the long day's travel broke into a trot.

Benita's brown face beamed at them from the doorway, and over her shoulder peered Juanita, with eyes only for Miguel.

Kitty had sunk immediately into one of the deep veranda chairs.

"I had to see how it feels to sit in a real live chair with a back once more," she explained. "And next I want to look at myself in a mirror that's more than three inches square; and have a drink out of a glass tumbler; and put on a clean white, fluffy dress!"

They each did all these things as eagerly as if they had been marooned on a desert island for many months; even Grandmother Clyde wearing fresh white linen, and Alec, for the first time on the ranch appearing in a starched shirt. Whereupon the girls broke into deafening applause.

"Letters, letters for everybody!" cried Blue Bonnet bursting into the living-room with a great bundle of mail. "Three for you and one for me, Grandmother,—postmarked Turino. Heaps for you, Kitty, ditto for Sarah, Amanda, Debby, Alec,—all Woodford must have joined in a round-robin. Hurry and read them and then everybody swap news!"

A long silence ensued, as profound as it was rare, while each girl pored over the precious home letters. It was Kitty who looked up first.

"Susy didn't catch the fever,—and Ruth's all over it. And she's had to have all her hair cut off, and she's dreadfully thin and doesn't seem to get her strength back as she should, Father says. He thinks she has fretted over having to miss the ranch party,—and no wonder!—it would simply have killed me. Susy's been a regular trump and hasn't complained a bit, but every one knows it's been a dreadful disappointment, especially when she was perfectly well and could have come if it hadn't been for Ruth."

"It's a downright shame!" Blue Bonnet declared.

"Father says if Ruth doesn't feel better soon she'll probably have to stay out of school this fall," Kitty continued.

"Then I should say she hadn't suffered in vain," exclaimed Blue Bonnet; Grandmother was deep in her letters.

"But think how mean it would be to have one of the We are Sevens out of school. You know how you love to 'have things complete,'" Amanda reminded her.

"Yes, but—" she began; then feeling her grandmother's eyes upon her, failed to finish. It was odd how the girls took it for granted that she was going back with them. And she was not at all sure, herself.

The girls had not noticed her hesitation, and were already exchanging other bits of home news and gossip. Alec alone was silent. Blue Bonnet, stealing a look at him saw that he had finished his letters and was staring moodily out of the window, unmindful of all the gay chatter about him.

"Did you get bad news, Alec?" she asked him, later that evening, as he accompanied her to the stable to see Texas and Massachusetts.

"That depends on the way you look at it. Boyd is coming back from Europe to take the West Point examinations—"

Blue Bonnet smothered an exclamation: she had seen that coming.

"—and Grandfather says that since the Army seems out of the question for me, he thinks I had better hurry home and take the Harvard exams. He seems set on it."

"And you don't want to?"

"It isn't to be thought of." Alec's mouth was very determined.

Now why, if West Point was disposed of, could he not take the next best—or in her opinion the very best—thing that offered? It was on the point of Blue Bonnet's tongue to put the question, when Alec spoke again.

"I've been putting off writing Grandfather,—what I told you a while ago,—thinking I might feel different after a time. But I'm more convinced than ever now. I had a long talk with Knight's friend 'Doc' Abbott, and he gave me a thorough going over, as he called it—"

"And what did he say?"

"He agrees with me, absolutely. There's no Harvard or any other college for Alec Trent—"

"Oh, Alec!" Blue Bonnet was trembling. To hide it she bent and picked up little Texas, stroking one of his silky ears. The coyotes had been placed in the empty rabbit-hutch, and were growing prodigiously.

"Well, it's better to know the truth and face it, isn't it?" Alec asked, as if rather resenting her tone.

"Yes, but—I can't see how you can speak so lightly about it. It's so dreadfully—serious."

"Lightly?" echoed Alec. "You're mistaken, Blue Bonnet. I know it's a mighty serious business for me. Why, if I could view it lightly, I could sit down and write Grandfather about it this very minute—"

"Well, if you don't, I'm going to!" she declared.

"Will you? Oh, Blue Bonnet, that's just what I've been hoping you'd do!" The relief in Alec's tone was unmistakable. "He's mighty fond of you, and I'm sure he'd consider that it came better from you than from me. And it will be a lot easier for you to do it, under the circumstances."

Easier! Blue Bonnet bent hastily and put Texas back in the bunny-house so that Alec might not see her face. If he had not been absorbed in his own thoughts he must have seen what a shock his words had been to her. It was so unlike Alec to put upon a girl a task he felt too hard for himself,—a sort of cowardice of which she would never have believed him capable. It took her some seconds to steady her voice before she could answer:

"I'll write to-morrow."

"You're a trump, Blue Bonnet! I seem to get deeper and deeper into your debt," he said earnestly.

Blue Bonnet fastened the little door of the rabbit-hutch, leaving Texas and Massachusetts to one of their frequent naps, and then walked back to the house in silence. Alec, observing her, believed her to be composing her letter to the General.

"The first of August to-day, just think how our summer is flying!" remarked Amanda next morning.

"Just three weeks to Blue Bonnet's birthday," said Sarah, who was engaged in making some mental calculations.

"Sixteen! Just think how old I'm getting!" Blue Bonnet's smile showed her not at all depressed at the prospect.

Uncle Joe cleared his throat gruffly. Why on earth did everybody keep harping on Blue Bonnet's growing up?

"I reckon you'll be having some howling celebration?" he asked rather crossly.

"You wager we will!" Uncle Cliff replied, all the more cheerfully because he guessed the reason for Uncle Joe's irritation. "A sixteenth birthday only comes once in a lifetime."

Mrs. Clyde, feeling an unusual sympathy with Uncle Joe, was silent.

"We must have some sort of a party that's—different," exclaimed Blue Bonnet.

"Everything's different in Texas," Sarah remarked, and the usual laugh followed.

"We can't have a dance without any boys," Blue Bonnet reflected.

"No boys?" exclaimed Uncle Joe, with a return of his twinkle, "Well, for a ranch that keeps a baker's dozen of cowboys—"

"All Mexicans except Sandy and Pete!" exclaimed Blue Bonnet scornfully.

"I'll agree to furnish a boy apiece for the festive occasion," said Uncle Cliff; and Blue Bonnet, exchanging a glance with him, knew he was nursing a well-laid scheme. "Now, listen," he continued. "I've been thinking over this thing—had time to think this last week!—and I've got it all figured out. My idea is to have an all-day affair, a real old-fashioned Spanish tournament."

Blue Bonnet clapped her hands. "Oh, Uncle Cliff, you do

think of the most glorious things!"

"In the morning," Uncle Cliff went on, "we could have a steer-roping contest—the Mexicans adore that—and Senorita Ashe bestow the prizes. And then—"

"Some bronco-busting," suggested Uncle Joe. Blue Bonnet turned pale and Uncle Cliff kicked his foreman under the table.

"None of that," he said briefly. "Too crude for our select company."

"A bull-fight, then," Uncle Joe persisted, "—that's Spanish, and the most seeleck ladies adore the ring."

"Oh, no!" cried Blue Bonnet, before she caught the gleam of mischief in the speaker's eye.

"We might have some races in the pasture," Alec suggested.

"Sure!" exclaimed Uncle Cliff. "And end with a grand fete in the evening,—and give everybody a holiday."

"Won't it be a great deal of work?" Mrs. Clyde inquired.

"Heaps. But these greasers never have enough to do,—we'll make them work for once," Mr. Ashe replied.

"What shall we wear?" Of course it was Kitty who asked.

"Oh, girls, I've the loveliest plan,—you don't mind, do you, Grandmother, if I get out my Spanish costume again?"

Grandmother smiled at a sudden recollection. "No, dear. I think it would fit this occasion admirably."

"But we haven't Spanish costumes!" said Debby and Amanda in a breath.

"Get them!" Blue Bonnet exclaimed. "Any old-fashioned, bright-colored gown will do to begin with, and a lace scarf for mantilla—"

"But where are we to get the gowns,—they don't grow on bushes," demanded Kitty.

"There is such a thing as a post, Kitty, and an express company. And you know your attics at home are full of lovely old things."

"Then we'll have to send right away to get them here in time."

The girls rose as if there were not a moment to lose, and, later in the day, Shady rode to Jonah with a well-filled mail-bag.

Blue Bonnet spent the entire morning over the composition of her letter to General Trent. When she sat down soberly to write Alec's grandfather a plain statement of facts, she found she had no facts to tell,—only a host of vague fears and hints that Alec had uttered from time to time. It was hardly to be wondered at, therefor, that her epistle when finished was pervaded with mystery of a veiled sort that made the General knit his brow, fall into a brown study, and then stalk off to the telegraph office.

It was Uncle Cliff who received the message and the matter aroused no comment. It said simply:

"With your permission will come to Texas. Arrive August twentieth. Prefer Alec should not know."

A telegram just as brief was despatched in reply; and no one was the wiser except Blue Bonnet and Grandmother Clyde. Blue Bonnet was much elated. Telling bad news at long range was something she did not approve of, and it promised to be a far easier solution of the problem to have the General see and learn for himself. It was not easy, however, to keep the matter from Alec, and Blue Bonnet, who had never had a secret of such importance before, had trouble more than once to keep from blurting it out.

The air for the next few days was full of mystery. Preparations for the birthday went forth apace, and the question of gifts was the important topic of the hour. Isolation from shops threw the girls largely upon their own resources; besides, it was known that Mrs. Clyde did not favor anything but the simplest of gifts. Sarah, whose drawn-work had progressed steadily in spite of all obstacles, enjoyed a small triumph, being the only one prepared with a suitable present.

"Now they'll leave me in peace while I finish it," she thought with a sigh of relief.

But it was not altogether peace that Sarah enjoyed, for the other girls took it into their heads to fashion something for Blue Bonnet with their own hands, and sought Sarah's room as the one spot secure from the eyes of the curious.

"What are you going to give Blue Bonnet?" Debby asked Alec one day.

He laughed mysteriously. "I'm aiming to surprise everybody as well as Blue Bonnet. It isn't much of a present, and the surprise is the only thing about it worth while."

Blue Bonnet was obligingly blind and deaf, in these days.

Letters flying back and forth, packages by mail or express, she ignored religiously.

"It's a real midsummer Christmas," she said to her grandmother one day, when all the other girls had shut themselves up in Sarah's room. "I thought there never could be anything so exciting and thrilly as getting ready for Christmas in Woodford, but this is running it close!"

"The mistress of the Blue Bonnet ranch is a very important personage these days," said Grandmother.

"She always has been made to feel important here. That's why it was so hard at first when I came to you and Aunt Lucinda." Blue Bonnet drew a low hassock beside her grandmother, and leaned cosily against her in the way they both loved. "You see, having my own way ever since I was old enough to have a way, didn't make it very easy to obey orders. My wishes didn't seem to count much with Aunt Lucinda."

"But they do count, dear. Your aunt is very fond of you, Blue Bonnet, and would grant any reasonable wish if she had it in her power."

"Oh, I understand her better now. It didn't take me very long to realize that she was running that ranch—that's a figure of speech, Grandmother,—and it was my turn *to be run*."

Mrs. Clyde stroked the brown head lovingly. "I saw the struggle, dear, and I know it was not easy. The things that are worth while don't come without effort."

Blue Bonnet smiled understanding into her grandmother's eyes. "I know. And I'm so glad I wasn't what Uncle Cliff calls a 'quitter.' Sticking it out was pretty hard, but it's made

C. E. Jacobs & Edyth Ellerbeck Read

me feel more—worthy, somehow, to be sixteen!"

Mystery reached its highest point the next day when Kitty, who had been absorbed in a bulky letter from home, suddenly gave a shrill scream of excitement, and summoning the other three girls, fled to Sarah's room. The high-pitched chatter and ejaculations that issued from that quarter made even Alec curious. Going around the house he hung on to the window-ledge and begged to be let into the secret.

"We want to surprise everybody!" said Debby revengefully.

Alec dropped to the ground and walked away in high amusement. Let them keep their secret then; he was sure he knew a surprise worth two of it. Then he betook himself to the Mexican quarters to note the progress of his own gift for Blue Bonnet.

CHAPTER XVIII

SOME ARRIVALS

THE birthday celebration really began on the day before the birthday. Uncle Cliff had driven to the railway station early in the day, and long before it was time for him to be back, five pairs of eyes began searching the road for a sight of the returning buckboard. The We are Sevens, observing Blue Bonnet to be as expectant as they, became apprehensive lest their great secret should have leaked out. For her part, Blue Bonnet had become so used to seeing the girls impatient for the arrival of the mail, that their frequent running to the veranda to peer down the road, occasioned her only amusement.

How little they suspected what a valuable package that buckboard would contain!

This was the twentieth of August. Every time Blue Bonnet thought of the great surprise in store for Alec, she grew first excited, then afraid. How would he take his grandfather's arrival? One minute she was sure he would be overwhelmingly glad, for Alec had a deep affection for the "grand old man." The next, she was afraid he would think she had shirked her bargain by throwing on him the burden of telling the General his own bad news. Well, this time she

C. E. Jacobs & Edyth Ellerbeck Read

had truly done her best, let the results be what they might.

"Do what is right let the consequence follow!" she sagely remarked to Solomon, and he put up his paw as if to say: "Shake on that!"

She was in her garden picking flowers for the table. Indoors was a delightful flurry of preparation: from the kitchen came a clatter of pans, and a variety of appetizing odors; above the cackle of Lisa and Gertrudis rang the merry laugh of Juanita as she waited on the busy cooks; while Miguel could be seen haunting the region of the back door.

Out on the long-disused croquet-ground, which Uncle Joe had levelled and tamped for Blue Bonnet years before, Alec and several of the cowboys were working, converting it into a dancing ground, and hanging Chinese lanterns on long wires strung between the surrounding trees.

"It's certainly worth while having a birthday on the ranch," Blue Bonnet thought happily. All this bustle of preparation to celebrate the birthday of a Texas Blue Bonnet!

Hark! Wasn't that the rattle of wheels? Yes,—there came the buckboard at last. Blue Bonnet sprang up excitedly. Had Alec heard? She shot a look in the direction of the croquet-ground.

Alec had heard; had glanced at the cloud of dust that marked the approaching team, and then—had gone calmly on with his work. He was looking for travellers on horseback, and the buckboard's arrival won only slight notice from him. He would let the girls spring their surprise on Blue Bonnet and have the hubbub over before he intruded.

"Alec!" called Blue Bonnet in a fever of excitement; but he

merely waved to her indulgently and went on fitting a candle into a socket with exasperating slowness.

With her arms full of flaming poppies, Blue Bonnet flew to the house and reached the veranda just as the other girls poured from the door, and the buckboard came to a standstill. There was the General, and beside him—Blue Bonnet gasped as she saw—was a boyish figure with close-cropped hair.

The poppies fell to the ground in a brilliant heap, and the moment that Susy and Ruth alighted Blue Bonnet gathered them both in an ecstatic hug. But not for long was she permitted a monopoly. These newly arrived two-sevenths were passed from hand to hand, or, more literally, from arm to arm, and caressed and exclaimed over until Mrs. Clyde came to the rescue of the tired girls.

The General's arrival had become of quite secondary importance. He stood talking to the Senora until Blue Bonnet at last turned to him apologetically.

"I'm very glad to see you!" she said.

General Trent took her outstretched hand and smiled down into the eager flushed face. "You are very good to say so. A mere man is decidedly *de trop* on such an occasion!"

"No, you're not! Only I was expecting you and I wasn't expecting Susy and Ruth,—so I rather lost my head. How did you happen to bring the girls?"

"I didn't bring them, really. Dr. Clark wanted them to have a change of air, and when Mrs. Doyle heard I was coming here she asked if I would mind playing escort to her girls,—a change of air spelt only Texas to them, it seems. My delight

may better be imagined than described, and—here we are.
Ah, Miss Kitty, you see me at last!" He paused to shake
hands with the young lady, and then the others came shyly
up with greetings.

"You didn't know I had a surprise up my sleeve, did you?"
Blue Bonnet challenged the girls.

"You must wear long sleeves!" laughed Kitty, tilting her chin
to look up at the tall military figure.

The General laughed with the rest but Blue Bonnet could see
him looking about with some impatience. "Where's Alec?"
he asked finally.

"We'll go find him. Take everybody indoors, will you,
Grandmother? I'll be back in a minute." Looking particularly
small and slight, Blue Bonnet moved off with her tall
companion towards the croquet-ground, where Alec, all
unconscious of their approach, stood on a step-ladder
adjusting one of the paper lanterns.

"How is the boy by this time?" General Trent asked.

"I—I don't know," Blue Bonnet stammered. It was quite true;
she had given up trying to guess the state of Alec's health.

The horizontal line between the General's eyes grew deeper:
it was plain that the girl shrank from telling him the worst.

Alec had started to descend the ladder when he caught sight
of the approaching pair. For a second he stood transfixed
with surprise; then with a real cowboy "whoop" of joy, took
a flying leap from his perch, cleared various obstacles with a
bound, and literally fell upon his grandfather.

"How splendid of you to come, sir!" was all he could exclaim for some minutes.

Finally the General took him by the shoulders and held him off, looking him over from head to foot. Blue Bonnet saw a look of incredulous wonder grow in his eyes, as he took in the increased breadth of the boy, the erect carriage and the red that glowed through the sunburn of his rounded cheeks.

"Why, boy, how you've grown!"

"Have I?" asked Alec eagerly. "Never felt so well before in all my life!"

Well? Blue Bonnet felt her face grow hot. How could Alec say that when he had let her—even urged her—to write that letter to his grandfather? If it was a joke, it struck her that Alec must have developed rather poor taste in jokes. She could feel the General's eyes upon her, questioning mutely. She could not meet his glance yet, and said with elaborate carelessness:

"I reckon you two would like to have a little talk, and the girls are waiting for me." She sped back to the house, and soon forgot her indignation in the joy of the We are Sevens' reunion.

"It seems too good to be true!" she exclaimed, gazing happily from one girl to another, as the seven of them lounged about the living-room, three on the broad couch and the rest distributed impartially between the floor and the window-seat. Such complete informality had never seemed permissible in the sedate Clyde mansion; but somehow these surroundings seemed to invite one to be as comfortable and unconventional as possible.

Suddenly Blue Bonnet's eyes danced. "Doesn't this remind you of my first tea-party?" she asked demurely.

"Well, I should say not!" Kitty exclaimed. "We all sat around your grandmother's drawing-room with manners as stiff as our dresses, waiting for our hostess—"

"And wondering what you would be like—" added Sarah.

"Were you prepared to see the wild Indian I proved to be?"

"Fishing!" sang Kitty.

Susy looked from Blue Bonnet to Kitty and laughed. "My, this sounds like old times!"

"Stop talking about old times, please," begged Ruth, "and tell us about the new ones. I want to be told all about the round-up, and I want to see the 'vast herds' and the cowboys,—and the blue bonnets!"

Blue Bonnet's laugh rang out. "Blue bonnets in August! Come in March and I'll show you a sea of them,—and a round-up, too. The cattle and the cowboys you shall see to-morrow,—and some steer-roping that will make your hair stand on end."

Ruth ran her hand through her boyish, close-cut locks and made them stand literally on end. "It isn't much of a trick to do that!" she said with a grimace.

"Never mind, maybe it will come in curly," said Sarah the comforter.

"You can trust Sarah not to see the thorns for the roses," said Blue Bonnet, sending the comforter an approving glance.

"What turtle doves you all are," laughed Susy.

"Oh, it's Sarah and Blue Bonnet who do all the cooing. The rest of us are still just geese." Kitty's voice had a tinge of envy that did not escape the notice of the rest.

"Go play us something, Blue Bonnet," suggested Ruth tactfully, "—that cowboy piece we all like."

"Invalids must be humored," remarked Blue Bonnet as she went to the piano.

In a minute the little rollicking air that she had played at her first tea-party, had set them all to dancing and humming as on that historic occasion.

"Aren't Kitty and Blue Bonnet as chummy as they used to be?" Ruth asked Amanda under cover of the music.

"Yes, by spells. They had one tiff—the second since they've known each other,—and ever since we've lived in dread of the third, haven't we, Sarah?"

"You have," Sarah returned. "And I have too, in fact, though I try not to be superstitious. Besides they've had the third— and it's all over now."

"They have? When?" Amanda sat up in surprise.

"While we were camping. Kitty told me about it and said it was all her fault. The last one wasn't, you know. First it's one and then the other that's to blame."

"Kitty and Blue Bonnet aren't going to stop at three tiffs, you may depend on it," Ruth said wisely. "They're going to have three times three and then some. Because Kitty is Kitty, and

Blue Bonnet is—Blue Bonnet!"

As the gay music ceased Grandmother Clyde looked in at the door. "It is time for the travellers to rest. They must be fresh for the great occasion to-morrow," she said, nodding to Susy and Ruth.

Blue Bonnet glanced over to the couch where Ruth reclined among the pillows. Her face, with its crown of short dark hair, looked very thin and white.

"I reckon the girls had better go to your room, Grand-mother,—it's about the only place where they can be quiet. Benita is putting two cots in the nursery, but it's never quiet in there till we're all asleep."

Ruth rose regretfully, "I'll go rest if I must. But I hate to miss anything that's going on. If you only knew how deadly dull it has been in Woodford! I think the inhabitants have learned to appreciate the We are Sevens, for the place has seemed empty without them. And everybody wants to know when the Texas Blue Bonnet is coming back."

They all looked towards Blue Bonnet. "I—why—there's Uncle Cliff looking for me," she said, and left the room precipitately.

"Blue Bonnet's usual way of avoiding an answer," thought Kitty.

"When does the Fall term of school begin?" asked Sarah.

"The tenth of September,—and that means we must leave here about the third," said Susy. "Only two weeks of this for us, girls!"

"We'll see that they are two busy weeks," Kitty promised.

Blue Bonnet drew Uncle Cliff into a secluded spot on the side veranda. "You just saved my life, Uncle Cliff."

"Were you being talked to death, Honey?"

"No,—but I just escaped a pitfall. People do ask the most— uncomfortable questions."

"Suppose you tell me what sort?"

"Well, Ruth says people want to know when the Texas Blue Bonnet is going back to Woodford."

"So that's come up again, eh?" Uncle Cliff knitted his brow. "I reckon you're doing some thinking along that line, Blue Bonnet?" He watched her face anxiously.

She nodded. "Yes, I—you see there isn't much time left. I must decide soon. It's not going to be easy, Uncle Cliff."

"No,—not for either of us, Honey."

"And there's Grandmother, too,—and Aunt Lucinda. Other people seem to have a lot to say about one's life, don't they?"

"They have a lot to say, Blue Bonnet, but the person who has the final 'say' is yourself. You're old enough now to decide what you want to do with your life. Sixteen to-morrow!"

"I know what I want to do with my life, Uncle, but I don't know yet just how to do it."

"Don't you think you could manage to do it on the ranch? We know now where to get a first-class tutor, and—"

"Oh, as far as 'book-learnin'"—as Uncle Joe calls it,—goes, I reckon I could get that all right, here on the ranch with a tutor. But books, I've found out, aren't more than half of an education. You know, life's mighty simple on the ranch, and I've grown used to doing things the easiest way. But that isn't the big way. Aunt Lucinda says every woman should have a vocation."

Uncle Cliff squirmed. Blue Bonnet seemed to have assimilated a rather big dose of Aunt Lucinda. "But, Honey," he protested, "a girl with plenty of money doesn't need a vocation."

"Oh, she didn't mean that kind of a vocation. It's a sort of glorified way of doing your duty by your neighbor. And you know it isn't very easy to do your duty by your neighbor when the nearest neighbor is miles away! Now, Aunt Lucinda is the most all-round useful person. She's helping to keep up a home for cripples in Boston, and is secretary of the Church Aid Society, runs Grandmother's house and—"

"Everybody in it!" added Uncle Cliff.

Blue Bonnet slipped her hand into his with a sympathetic pressure.

"I reckon I caught it from you,—liking to paddle my own canoe, I mean. But, though I don't love discipline, I've learned to appreciate what it can do. Now, look at Solomon—"

"—in all his glory!" laughed Uncle Cliff.

At that moment the subject of the conversation was occupied in gnawing a very dirty bone on the forbidden territory of the veranda.

"Oh, he has his lapses," Blue Bonnet confessed, "—his forgettery is as active as mine. But he's hardly more than a puppy yet, and it's surprising how well he minds. He's getting pretty wild out here. The ranch has that effect I've observed. And that's why—"

"Say, Honey," Uncle Cliff interrupted, "let's allow the subject of going back to rest right where it is until after to-morrow, will you? I want to enjoy my ward's birthday, and I'd rather have a clear sky without any clouds on my horizon."

"That suits me, Uncle Cliff."

"And while we're on the subject of the birthday, there's something I want to tell you, Blue Bonnet. I know it's usual to keep one's gift a secret, but—"

"Oh, I hope it's just some simple thing, Uncle. Grandmother's been looking pretty serious lately over what she thinks is our extravagant way of living. The Woodford girls have to be very careful about expenses, you know, and she thinks it makes it harder for them to be satisfied when they see me have so much."

"Don't you worry, young lady. I'm only taking a leaf out of your book, and instead of giving pleasure to just one person—i. e. Blue Bonnet Ashe,—I'm going to distribute it over quite a crowd. The trouble is it won't keep till to-morrow. It's about due now. Jump on Firefly, will you, and ride with me to meet it?"

"Yes, everybody is resting, or supposed to be. Just wait till I slip on my riding-skirt and I'll be with you."

A few minutes later Blue Bonnet and her uncle, after the

C. E. Jacobs & Edyth Ellerbeck Read

fashion of the old days, cantered down the road together.

Hardly had they disappeared when Kitty, also attired in riding-costume, stole quietly to the stable, and having found one of the Mexicans to saddle Rowdy, rode briskly out of the corral and off to the woods across San Franciscito.

At the gate Uncle Cliff drew rein. "We'd better form a reception committee right here. I think I hear your birthday present coming."

Blue Bonnet looked down the road expectantly. What could it be?

Then, as they waited, there came the rhythmic pound of hoofs, a cloud of dust, and suddenly there swept into sight a company of riders with Knight and Carita in the lead.

"Oh, Uncle Cliff, what a splendid birthday present!" And Blue Bonnet, with a glad "Ho ye, ho ho!" of welcome, galloped to meet the procession.

Sandy and the three "props of the world"—Smith, Brown and Jones, with two of the younger boys from camp—made, as Uncle Cliff had promised, a "boy apiece" for the We are Sevens and Carita; and the entire party, dusty though they were from the long ride, were incorrigibly cheerful and apparently not at all tired by the trip.

"Oh, I'm so happy!" cried Carita, as Blue Bonnet fell in beside her and led the way to the ranch. "I never dreamed I could come. But Mr. Ashe had made all arrangements, and Mother said she could get along without me for the three days,—she's going to stay at the Camp. Just think, if we hadn't gone up there again, I couldn't have known about it in time!"

"How lucky! Carita, I think you are the nicest birthday present that was ever thought of."

Carita looked up in surprise.

"Having you and Knight and the boys here is my birthday gift from Uncle," Blue Bonnet explained. "Wasn't it down-right grand of him to plan it?"

"It's sweet of you to want us," Carita returned. "And your uncle looks as if he loved to do nice things. He has the kindest eyes I've ever seen."

"Except your father's," Blue Bonnet added. "I think they must both have been cut out by the same pattern."

Alec, who was in the secret, had assembled everybody on the veranda awaiting the arrivals, and the hubbub that ensued as the cavalcade dismounted and everybody exchanged greetings, convinced Susy, Ruth and the General that life in Texas was quite as exciting as it had been painted.

Mrs. Clyde, having been prepared by Uncle Cliff for this invasion, tried to view the proceedings as a matter of course, and was her usual cordial self.

"Where are we going to put them all?" Blue Bonnet asked in an undertone.

"Shady and Uncle Joe put up a tent as soon as you rode off," her grandmother explained. "The boys are used to camping out and there are only two nights to plan for. Carita can share Sarah's room. Lisa has enlarged the dining-room table, and we shall have room for all. I hope we can make our guests comfortable."

"Don't you worry, Grandmother. These guests will make the best of everything. People out here don't expect things to be—orderly, as they are in Woodford."

"Evidently not!" was Grandmother's unspoken thought.

"Where's Kitty?" asked Blue Bonnet presently, missing one saucy face from the group on the side veranda where they had all gathered.

"Didn't she go with you? We haven't seen her for an hour or more," replied Sarah.

"Here she comes now." Alec rose and went to assist Kitty from her horse. "Hello, Miss Unsociable," he said. "Fancy riding all by your lones! Been keeping a tryst?"

"Nothing so romantic," she confessed. "I've been gathering these lovely wild vines to decorate the table with. See how pretty they are!" She tossed the big armful of glossy green stuff down to him. To her surprise and indignation Alec dodged her offering and let the vines fall in a heap on the ground. Kitty paused in the act of dismounting and stared at him, speechless with surprise at this act from well-bred Alec.

"I beg your pardon, Kitty," he laughed. "I didn't mean to be rude, but I'm deadly afraid of that stuff."

"Stuff!" echoed Kitty. She was off her horse in a minute, and giving the reins to Miguel who had come up for Rowdy, she bent to pick up her insulted treasure.

Alec prevented her. "I wouldn't, Kitty,—though I don't suppose it matters now. The mischief's done, I'm afraid,— that's poison ivy."

"Poison ivy!" Kitty sprang back as if the vine were about to sting her. "I never saw any before,—and I wanted to surprise Blue Bonnet—it looked so pretty. Oh, Alec, are you sure?"

"Sure?—positive. Dr. Judson pointed out lots of it around Camp, and we learned to give it a wide berth. But say, every one isn't susceptible, Kitty. Maybe you're immune."

"Oh, dear!" wailed Kitty. "What shall I do? Can't I be vaccinated or something to ward it off?"

"What's the trouble?" asked Uncle Joe, coming up in time to hear Kitty's despairing cry.

"Poison ivy," said Alec, pointing to the vines.

"Now that's bad." Uncle Joe kicked the innocent looking heap of greens off to one side. "I'll send up one of the boys to rake that up and get rid of it. Nasty stuff to have around,—'specially for folks with your—coloring." He eyed Kitty's milk-white freckled face apprehensively.

"If I get it and have to miss the party I'll never get over it!" Kitty declared.

"Oh, yes, you will—it only lasts a few days, generally," said Uncle Joe.

Kitty dabbed her eyes with her handkerchief.

"Here—don't do that!" Alec exclaimed hastily. "That might play the mischief with your eyes. Go bathe your face and hands with witch hazel, that may help. And hurry out again, Kitty—your friend Sandy is on the side veranda."

Kitty for the first time glanced towards the house and saw

C. E. Jacobs & Edyth Ellerbeck Read

the latest arrivals. "Carita, too! Have they come to the party? Oh, what fun! That's what Mr. Ashe meant when he promised us a boy apiece for the dance. But oh, Alec—what if—?" Kitty could not finish.

"Please don't get it, Kitty,—it would spoil the day for Sandy!"

CHAPTER XIX

BLUE BONNET'S BIRTHDAY

"SIXTEEN to-day!" was Blue Bonnet's first thought as she opened her eyes next morning.

Could it be only a year since her last birthday? Less than a year since she had first seen Grandmother? Why, it seemed now as if she must have known Grandmother and Aunt Lucinda all her life! She tried to remember how she used to feel before she ever left the ranch; before she had ever seen Woodford, or the We are Sevens, or—but the list seemed interminable; she gave up trying to recall how the Blue Bonnet of that careless time had thought and felt and spent her days.

Was every year to bring as many new experiences, as many new faces into her life? Surely not if she stayed on the ranch, and if she went—But Uncle Cliff had said that question was to be banished for this day.

Rising and dressing noiselessly, she stole out of the nursery for one of her usual early morning romps. Being sixteen should not rob her of the right to be a child at this hour of the day!

"Wish me many happy returns, Solomon!" she cried as the dogs raced to her across the yard. "Don, this is the fifth occasion of this sort you've attended,—you're getting on in years, too. Come on, I'll race you to the fence!"

Uncle Cliff watched her from the pasture, a chuckle of satisfaction escaping him at this evidence of untamed tomboyism. He met her as she came up flushed and breathless.

"Getting mighty dignified since you turned sixteen, aren't you?"

Her laughing face peered at him over the rough old logs. "Not so you'd notice it!"

"I reckon I ought to thump you sixteen times and one to grow on. But that would make it necessary to climb the fence. How would you like kisses instead?"

"Give me the big one to grow on, anyway." She held up her lips. "And now I must run in to Grandmother,—she must have the next."

She found the Senora waiting for her in the living-room.

"I'm so glad you're alone, Grandmother. I wanted you all to myself for a minute or two." She went straight into the arms Grandmother held out to her, was folded close for a moment and received a second kiss "to grow on."

"While we're alone I want to tell you something," Blue Bonnet said earnestly, "—about this last year, I mean. I never have said just what I've felt. It has been the best of all years, Grandmother, and the best of all the good things it has brought me—is you."

"Thank you, dear. And you must know, Blue Bonnet, without my telling you how great a comfort you are to me."

"Truly, Grandmother,—a comfort?"

"Beyond words, dear." And Grandmother gave her another kiss to grow on. "And now, Blue Bonnet, here is something for your birthday."

Blue Bonnet took the dainty package and unwrapped it with fingers that trembled a little. Within the paper was a box, and inside that, looking out from a frame of dull Roman gold, was her mother's face. It was an exquisite miniature, painted on ivory. The rose-tints of the flesh and the deep tender blue of the eyes that smiled up at her, made the portrait seem a living thing. Blue Bonnet could not speak. She gazed and gazed at the dear features until her eyes blurred and she had to put up her hand to brush the tears away.

"Oh, Grandmother—!" Her lip quivered and she could say no more.

But Grandmother understood.

"Your aunt had it done from a photograph while she was in Rome. The painter was a Boston woman—an old friend of ours who knew your mother, Blue Bonnet. That is why the coloring is so true. The eyes are your eyes—can't you see, dear?"

"Am I truly like her?"

"So like, Blue Bonnet, that sometimes it seems as if Elizabeth had never left me."

"I'm glad, Grandmother. Oh, how I shall treasure this! How

can I ever thank you and Aunt Lucinda? There come the others,—I think I won't show them this just now. I'd rather let them see it one at a time. Somehow a crowd—"

"I understand, Blue Bonnet."

It was well that she and her grandmother had made the most of that quiet five minutes before breakfast; for it was the last peaceful moment that day.

As all the gay party trooped into the dining-room with its long table looking like a real banquet board, a big floral decoration was the first thing to greet all eyes. A long low basket of closely woven fibres formed a centrepiece, and inside it, growing so densely that only a vivid mass of blue showed above the brim, were blue bonnets in bloom.

"How sweet! Where did they come from?" Blue Bonnet demanded, looking from face to face.

"There's a card on the handle," some one suggested.

Blue Bonnet bent and read: "Blue Bonnet's namesakes wish her many happy returns of the day." Looking up she caught Alec's eye. "You?" she asked.

"Guilty!" he confessed.

"You clever boy! You couldn't have given me anything I should love as much. How did you ever do it?"

"Easy enough. Planted the seeds and took care of them,—had a bad scare for fear they wouldn't bloom in time. I've had them back of Marta's cabin and she's been sitting up nights with them!"

They all crowded about the table for a closer view.

"I'm so glad we can see some blue bonnets before leaving. That's been the one thing necessary to complete Texas!" exclaimed Kitty.

"Sure you don't mean ivy?" asked Alec in an undertone.

She wilted. "Sh! Please don't remind me of that,—I was almost happy again!"

"No symptoms yet?" he asked.

"None—yet. I live in hopes!"

"Let's wait till after breakfast before we give Blue Bonnet our gifts," suggested Sarah. "She'll enjoy them more, I think."

"Not to mention our enjoyment!" laughed Kitty.

The suggestion was followed, and at the conclusion of the meal, Blue Bonnet kept her seat and opened the rest of her packages with the eyes of all the crowd upon her. Very simple were the gifts, as the Woodford girls had slender purses; but the love and good will that went with the presents made up for their lack of material value.

From Kitty there was a dainty sewing apron of muslin, with pretty blue bows on the pockets; from Amanda, a fancy-work bag, and from Debby a complicated needlecase. A silver thimble from Susy and Ruth completed these very feminine accessories.

Alec's eyes twinkled as Blue Bonnet tried the thimble on her slender finger-tip. "If you're not a model of industry after this, Blue Bonnet, it will prove you're rather slow at taking a hint!"

The girls joined heartily in the laugh against them, though they professed entire innocence of any such intention as Alec implied.

Sarah's gift provoked a chorus of exclamations. From the fine drawn-work, the hand-made tucks, to the tiny irreproachable buttonholes, the waist was a triumph of the needlewoman's art.

"It's the prettiest one I ever had!" Blue Bonnet declared. She would have liked to jump up and kiss Sarah, the dear old thing! But with eight boys looking on, such a demonstration might appear done for effect, she concluded; and so reserved that mark of affection for a future occasion.

When the girls had presented their offerings, Knight came up and dropped a paper parcel into her lap. On the card tied to the blue ribbon that decorated it was written: "To the Good Samaritan from the One Who Fell by the Wayside." There was a laugh in Knight's eyes as he watched her read the inscription and then unwrap the tissue-paper that enclosed the object.

Blue Bonnet lifted the lid of the long narrow box, took one look, and met Knight's eyes with an answering laugh in her own. Inside the box was a shimmering red silk sash. Knight had kept his promise to himself to buy Blue Bonnet the "fanciest thing in the sash line that Chicago could boast"— even though it had taken the last penny of his pocket money.

"It's a beauty!" she declared.

"Knight must expect another spill to-day," laughed Alec.

Blue Bonnet looked about the circle with a bright, quick glance. "I'm not going to try to say 'thank you' to every-body,—those two words would be quite worn out by the time I finished!"

"Come along, everybody," said Uncle Cliff, "it's time for the festivities to begin."

As they left the dining-room, Carita slipped her arm about Blue Bonnet and whispered regretfully: "I wish I had a present for you. I didn't know in time or I could have made something."

Blue Bonnet gave her an impulsive squeeze. "Why, Carita, you're a birthday present yourself!"

Blue Bonnet's promise to Ruth in regard to the steer-roping contest, proved almost literally true. This was the great feature of the day to the Mexicans, and their delight in the sport knew no bounds. They made a brilliant picture as they stood or squatted about the corral gate, the women in their bright yellow, red and purple calicoes; and the men in their tight trousers, serapes rainbow hued, gay sashes and enormous peaked hats. The scene was full of life, color and motion.

Ruth's thin cheeks grew pink with excitement. "What's going to happen first?" she asked Blue Bonnet.

"You see those steers inside the gate? Well, Pancho will drive one out and while it is running like mad, Josef—he has the first turn—will lasso, throw it, and tie its feet together with that short rope he has. Then, one after another, the rest of the cowboys will do the same thing, and the one that does it in the shortest time will get the prize and be declared champion of the Blue Bonnet ranch."

C. E. Jacobs & Edyth Ellerbeck Read

"The world's record is thirty-seven seconds," Knight added, "but it has to be a hustler who can do it under a minute."

"Look—there comes one now!" screamed Kitty.

The contest was swift, breathless and soon over. The corral gate was opened and through it driven a steer. Outside, mounted on a swift cow-pony rode Josef, awaiting the signal to start in pursuit. On came the steer with long frightened leaps, after him the vaquero with lariat whirling around his head. Suddenly the rope whistled, hissed through the air, dropped and coiled about the steer's front feet. A quick movement on the part of both rider and horse; the lariat tightened, and the steer pitched on to its side. Josef leaped from his pony, bent over his victim, and, in far less time than it takes to tell it, had tied three of the kicking hoofs together. The cowboy rose, grinning, amid the cheers of the delighted audience; and remounting his horse, coolly rolled a cigarette.

"Sixty-three seconds," said Knight, who was time-keeper.

One after another the cowboys took their turns, and every fraction of a second shaved from Josef's record, sent the Mexicans wild with excitement. It was Lupe who was finally declared champion, and received from Blue Bonnet's hands the silver-braided Mexican sombrero that was the prize.

"I wonder why Miguel didn't try," Blue Bonnet remarked, as Lupe walked proudly away with his trophy. "He's always been able to beat Lupe."

"I asked Pancho where Miguel was," said Alec, "and he said no one had seen him to-day. Maybe Juanita objects to steer-roping!" They smiled with a secret understanding.

"How do you like the sport?" Blue Bonnet asked, turning

to Ruth.

"It's exciting,—but isn't it cruel, Blue Bonnet?"

"I reckon the steer thinks so," Blue Bonnet confessed. "But the cowboys have to practise, you know, for at the round-up that's the way they have to throw the calves to brand them."

"Then I don't want to see a round-up!" Ruth declared.

Next came races in the pasture, and in these the girls and boys were the contestants. Blue ribbons were the awards pinned on the winners by Blue Bonnet herself, and the rivalry for them was intense. Leaning against the pasture fence which formed the "grandstand" General Trent, Uncle Cliff, Uncle Joe, Mrs. Clyde, Susy, Ruth and Blue Bonnet watched and applauded; while the Mexicans, squatting about in characteristic attitudes, chattered and laughed like a lot of children.

As Sarah swept by on Comanche to take her place at the starting-line, Ruth and Susy turned amazed and questioning eyes on Blue Bonnet. She laughed at their expressions of wonder.

"Keep your eye on Sarah!" she bade them. "Comanche is one of the swiftest horses on the ranch, and he and our Sallykins are on the best of terms."

To Blue Bonnet's secret delight Sarah won the first race. As she pinned the blue ribbon to the winner's middy blouse, her own face beamed the triumph that Sarah was too modest to betray.

"Aren't you going in for any others?" Ruth asked, as Sarah returned on foot and dropped on the blanket beside her.

C. E. Jacobs & Edyth Ellerbeck Read

"No, I only rode in that race to keep the girls from calling me 'fraid-cat.' I'm sure Father wouldn't approve of horse-racing."

Ruth laughed. "You are the same old Sarah! I was beginning to believe that the Blue Bonnet ranch had bewitched you."

"Don't say 'bewitched,'" Blue Bonnet interrupted, "locoed is the word we use in Texas."

The birthday dinner, served early as was the custom at the ranch, was the most animated of feasts, of which the birthday-cake with its sixteen blazing candles was the grand climax. It was fat Lisa herself who waddled in and deposited her masterpiece in front of the Senorita, and then lingered to see how it looked after cutting.

"It's divine, Lisa,—a complete success!" Blue Bonnet cried, and the cook grinned delightedly. As Lisa turned to leave the room, Blue Bonnet detained her to whisper—"Why is Benita waiting on table alone?—where's Juanita?"

"Who knows?" returned Lisa with a shrug of her massive shoulders. "That *nina* is run off and Gertrudis means to thrash her."

"Oh, Lisa, she mustn't!" Blue Bonnet said in genuine distress. "Tell Gertrudis I'll come out and see her after dinner."

She found Gertrudis slamming about the dishes in a most reckless fashion and muttering to herself angrily. To Blue Bonnet's plea in behalf of the absent Juanita she returned only stormy answers.

"No, Senorita, she is spoiled for lack of thrashing. Run off on the Senorita's birthday! With a horde to wait on! And enough work for fifty lazy things like herself!"

No, Juanita should be thrashed if ever she could lay hands on her. Blue Bonnet could not sway her from her purpose, and finally gave up arguing and left the kitchen, vowing mentally to prevent the angry old woman from carrying out her threat. But in the excitement of the evening's festivities, she forgot all about it.

What an evening it was! Not one of the boys and girls lucky enough to be there would ever forget the scene. The broad verandas on which half the furniture of the house had been brought to form cosy-corners and lounging places; the soft gleam of Chinese lanterns strung among the trees; the music of Shady's violin, augmented by a flute and cello from Jonah, to which they danced on the croquet-ground; and everywhere the We are Sevens, stately in trains and hair dressed high, tripping and laughing and flirting their fans in the manner fondly believed to be that of high-born Spanish dames.

Susy and Ruth had obligingly crammed their trunks with the attic treasures of the various Woodford families, and the costumes, while not strictly Spanish, were quite gorgeous and "partified" enough to satisfy these finery-loving young folk. Among them they had managed to fit out Carita too, and she, in a yellow gown with velvety gold-of-Ophir roses in the dusky coils of her hair, looked like a real maid of Andalusia. Blue Bonnet, in her red satin gown, which had not seen the light since the night it had been worn for the benefit of the Boston relatives, was a picture.

Alec came up to her in the middle of the evening and made a low bow. "Senorita Blue Bonnetta, you look charming to-night, but it strikes me you're carrying things with a high hand. Why, among all your humble subjects, am I not favored with a dance or promenade? You've been engaged three deep every time I've asked you."

For a minute Blue Bonnet toyed with her fan without speaking. She had purposely avoided Alec for a reason she considered good and sufficient. There was an explanation due her from him, and that also, she was resolved, should be "good and sufficient" or she would not accept it. And it seemed best, if there was to be any clash between them, that it should not come on her birthday. She would not easily forgive him for urging her to write that letter to the General.

As she hesitated and a surprised look crept into Alec's eyes, there came a great outcry from the direction of Marta's cabin,—shouts, cheers and bursts of laughter.

"The Mexicans must be doing stunts,—let's go and see," Alec suggested.

Gathering up her train Blue Bonnet hurried with him to the Mexican quarters, where the noisy crowd had assembled. Half way there they met Gertrudis, also headed for the scene of merriment.

"It's that Juanita, they say," she cried, "come back after all the work's done!" Her swarthy face was dark with anger; in her hand was a willow switch.

"Hurry!" cried Blue Bonnet. "Let's get there first, Alec,—she means to thrash Juanita!"

Running and tripping on her long dress Blue Bonnet reached the group and at her appearance the Mexicans burst into renewed cheering.

"The Senorita!" they cried and parted to make room for her.

"What is it—what's all the noise about?" asked Alec.

But, as the circle parted, revealing a tableau in the centre, he and Blue Bonnet needed no explanation. Standing hand in hand, in attitudes expressing both embarrassment and triumph, were—Miguel and Juanita.

"Ran off to Jonah and got married!" chuckled Pinto Pete.

Blue Bonnet and Alec gazed at each other in stupefaction for a second, then Blue Bonnet glanced hastily about for Gertrudis. The change in the old woman was instantaneous. She turned to Blue Bonnet with a grin.

"That Miguel makes good wages!" she cried. The anger had faded from her face, and instead of the switch, Juanita received her blessing.

"What a mercenary old thing Gertrudis is!" exclaimed Blue Bonnet, as, after congratulating the happy pair, she and Alec walked back to the house.

"She's a sensible woman," Alec remarked provokingly. "Most of the Mexicans are lazy old loafers,—but Miguel has a streak of real American industry."

"Well," said Blue Bonnet, "I little expected my birthday party to be turned into a wedding!"

When the last candle had been blown out and all was quiet except for the echo of music and laughter from the Mexican quarters, where the wedding festivities were continued almost till dawn, Blue Bonnet slipped into her grandmother's room for a last word before retiring.

"The sixteenth has been the best birthday of all," she said happily. "Are you quite tired out, Grandmother?"

C. E. Jacobs & Edyth Ellerbeck Read

And Mrs. Clyde, bending to kiss the glowing face upturned to her, replied: "No, dear. It has been a beautiful party. But I'm glad for all our sakes that Blue Bonnet Ashe has but one birthday a year!"

CHAPTER XX

CONFERENCES

IT was well on towards noon before any one in either the house or tent was stirring. Blue Bonnet and Ruth were the first to open their eyes, and they carried on a conversation in whispers for some time before waking the others.

Ruth looked around the six beds in the nursery and smiled. "It looks like a ward in a hospital, doesn't it?"

"Pretty healthy looking invalids in them," Blue Bonnet replied. "Look what red cheeks Kitty has."

Ruth raised herself and leaned on one elbow, peering at the unconscious Kitty. "Red as fire. Doesn't she look funny?"

"Makes her hair look pale!" laughed Blue Bonnet. All at once, as she studied the face that looked a brilliant scarlet against the white pillow, the smile faded from her face. "Ruth, come here," she said in a queer tone.

Ruth obediently stole from her bed and tiptoed to Blue Bonnet's side.

"Look at Kitty *hard*."

C. E. Jacobs & Edyth Ellerbeck Read

"Doesn't she look strange?" Ruth whispered.

A sudden thought made Blue Bonnet start. "Ruth, were you fumigated before you left Woodford?"

"Fumigated? Goodness no! They fumigate houses, not people."

"Well, disinfected is what I mean, I reckon. Kitty's got a rash—and it's scarlet!"

They gazed at each other in dismay. Kitty stirred, moaned, and sat up.

"What are you all talking about?—oh, girls,—I can't open my eyes!"

At her cry all the other occupants of the nursery woke up, and crowded about the anguished Kitty.

"Oh, Susy, look at her," cried Blue Bonnet. "Did Ruth look like that? Do you think it's scarlet fever?"

"Scarlet fever nothing!" wailed Kitty. "It's poison ivy, that's what it is!"

"How can it be? What makes you think so?" Blue Bonnet demanded.

Kitty's tale was soon told, and to her indignation it provoked a laugh.

"It's no laughing matter, I tell you," she exclaimed miserably.

"You wouldn't say that if you could see yourself!" Blue Bonnet returned.

"You wouldn't think it so funny if both your eyes were swollen shut and your face burned like fire." Kitty tried to look pathetic, but only succeeded in looking funnier than ever.

Stifling their laughter, but exchanging glances of amusement every time they caught sight of Kitty's blotched and swollen countenance, the girls dressed and went to seek advice for the sufferer. Everything in the shape of a remedy from soap-suds to raw beefsteak was proposed by somebody or other, and nearly every one of them tried before the day was over. Kitty kept her bed and Sarah constituting herself nurse, ministered unto the afflicted one.

It was hard for fun-loving Kitty to be shut up in a darkened room with her eyes and face bandaged, while the sounds of merriment and laughter floated tantalizingly in. Sarah was kept busy bearing the numerous messages of sympathy, ranging from the sublime to the ridiculous, that Sandy and some of the other boys spent their time in composing.

It was decided that the party from Camp Judson should remain over until the next day, since all had risen too late for the desired early start. Carita looked supremely happy when Knight yielded to Blue Bonnet's arguments and reached this decision. She had so wanted to stay, and yet—there were so many reasons why she should go; and it was a great relief to her conscience to have Knight assume all responsibility for their prolonged visit.

"Now maybe we can have another nice talk," she said, sinking down beside Blue Bonnet in the hammock on the side veranda. "We've had only snatches, so far. And it will be so long before I see you again."

"What makes you think so?" Blue Bonnet asked rather abruptly.

250   C. E. Jacobs & Edyth Ellerbeck Read

"Why,—you will be leaving in two weeks, the girls said."

"Oh, they did." Blue Bonnet was thoughtful for a moment, then burst out—"Carita, what would you do, if you were in my place,—about going back East again?"

"What would I do?" Carita repeated wonderingly. "Why, Blue Bonnet, do you mean that you're not sure about going?"

"I do mean—just that. The girls have taken it for granted all along that I was going back with them, but somehow I can't make up my mind. Every day the ranch grows dearer. And being shut up in a stuffy schoolroom, and having to get up and go to bed by the clock, and having a place for everything and everything in its place—Carita, it goes against the grain!"

Carita gave a comical little sigh. "It's queer how things seem to be—cut on the bias, isn't it? Now to go to school, and see and know lots of people, and have libraries and hear music— why, I seem sometimes to *ache* for it all."

"It's a pity you're not Aunt Lucinda's niece. You'd do her credit. Now the only person I seem to suit through and through, is Uncle Cliff. He's been father and mother both to me, and I think that I owe him something in return. I can't bear to leave him all alone again."

"I know. I should feel just that way about Mother. She needs me, but, if we could afford it, she'd be the first to send me away to school. If I could get enough education to teach, I could help her more in the end."

"I reckon it's the end that makes everything endurable. It was the thought of getting back to the ranch that got me through last year. But I haven't let myself think what the end of this summer would bring. Every day on the ranch is complete in itself."

"But think how it will seem after this—when the girls are all gone, and your grandmother—"

"It's Grandmother who counts more than any one, except Uncle Cliff. I reckon I'll just have to be blindfolded and then choose!"

"There come Knight and Alec," said Carita. "I shouldn't wonder if they'd been having the same sort of a conversation. They'd like to change places with each other. Knight is wild to go East to college, and Alec would give anything for—"

"Knight's health and strength,—I know," Blue Bonnet interrupted. "It's another case of the mixed-upness of things. I'm disappointed in Alec."

Carita opened her eyes wide. "Disappointed? Why, I should think you, of all people, feeling as you do, would sympathize with him."

"I do sympathize with him, and always have. That's why I was so glad Uncle Cliff asked him out here. I was sure it would do him the world of good—"

"And so it has," said Carita. "It has done wonders for him, Knight says, and that's why—"

"And that's why I don't understand how he could possibly—" Blue Bonnet broke off as the subject of their conversation took the three veranda steps in one leap and settled himself comfortably on the railing for a chat. Knight threw himself into a chair near the hammock.

"What are you two plotting?" asked Alec. "You've had your heads together like a pair of Russian conspirators."

"We're only trying to make the most of every minute we're together. At least that's what I'm doing," said Carita. "I believe you two are doing very much the same thing."

The boys smiled at each other: that was a girl's way of putting it, but it came very near the truth.

"I reckon you two girls will have lots to write about this winter," said Knight. "Carita used to wonder, all last year, how you looked, and what the We are Sevens were like, and what you all wore and did and ate and—" He broke off with a laugh at Carita's indignant denial. "I expect her mind will be in Woodford more than ever, after this."

"But Blue Bonnet may not go back," Carita began, when a look from Blue Bonnet checked her.

"Not go back?" In his surprise Alec nearly fell off the railing. "Here's news for the We are Sevens! Well, Blue Bonnet, I can't say I'm sorry." So far from being depressed at the prospect, Alec looked highly elated.

Blue Bonnet was strangely still. Alec had said that very much as if he meant it. And it hurt. After almost a year of close friendship it was, to say the least, hardly good taste to pretend he was glad she was no longer going to live next door to him. She did not intend, however, to let him see how she felt, and rose without glancing in his direction.

"I must go see Kitty," she said briefly.

Alec looked after her with a perplexed expression in his eyes. "Isn't Blue Bonnet a bit offish lately, Carita? She doesn't seem at all like herself."

"I think she's worried," said Carita. "It is hard trying to please both her uncle and her grandmother, when one wants her in Massachusetts, and the other urges her to stay on the ranch."

"So that's the trouble?" Alec looked somewhat relieved.

"Poor Blue Bonnet must feel rather like the rag we saw Texas and Massachusetts worrying this morning," laughed Knight, "each took a corner and pulled!"

"She ought to appreciate one fact," added Alec, "and that is, she at least can decide for herself. She isn't compelled to do what somebody else decides for her."

"Just the same, I believe she would prefer having some one else do it," said Carita.

In spite of Carita's explanation, Alec was not wholly at ease in his mind about Blue Bonnet. He imagined that her manner to him for the last few days had conveyed a vague reproach. But he had no chance that day to talk with her alone.

Early the next morning Carita and Knight and the other boys prepared for the long ride back to Camp Judson.

"You'll write me soon, Blue Bonnet, won't you, and tell me what you decide to do?" Carita asked as she leaned down from her pinto for a last word with Blue Bonnet.

"Indeed I will," Blue Bonnet assured her. "I wish I knew now."

"And you'll write often if you go back—all about school and

the girls and—"

"I'll write about everything, if—!"

And this was the word on which they parted.

Sandy lingered behind the others long enough to slip an envelope into Blue Bonnet's hand. "For Kitty," he explained. "Tell her I'm mighty sorry I couldn't see her to say good-bye."

"Maybe it is only '*hasta la vista*,' as the Spanish say,—'good-bye till we meet again,'" said Blue Bonnet. "You must surely come to Woodford and see us if you go to Harvard."

"'Neither foes nor loving friends'—shall hinder me from doing that same, if—!"

And with this word, Sandy, too, galloped after the others.

Alec was to accompany the boys as far as the ford. As he rode away on Strawberry, looking very straight and manly in the saddle, General Trent gazed after him with an expression of pride in his eyes.

"The change in the boy is hardly short of marvellous, Miss Blue Bonnet," he said at last, turning to her. "I should never have believed it if I had not seen him. I'm very grateful to you for writing me that letter, though I confess you had me badly puzzled."

Blue Bonnet had stood looking regretfully after Carita, but at the General's words she turned with a brightened face. If he was grateful, then he must have forgiven her for bringing him to Texas on what was evidently an unnecessary errand.

"I was afraid you might think I had—rushed in," she said.

"Not at all!" he replied. "Though I did not quite understand—you weren't entirely clear, you know."

Indeed she did know!

"But Alec has explained the situation," the General continued, "and I understand everything now."

Blue Bonnet drew a quick breath of relief. "Then it's all right?"

"Yes,—and he need not have hesitated. I sympathize with him wholly."

Sympathize? How queerly he said it. Again Blue Bonnet was swept out to sea.

"I am going to talk with Mr. Ashe about the matter now. We must do what is best for the boy." As General Trent walked to meet Uncle Cliff, Blue Bonnet stood staring after him, her thoughts in a whirl.

"What's the matter? You look as if you had just been through an earthquake," laughed Ruth, coming up and slipping her thin hand into Blue Bonnet's.

"I think I have,—and everything is upside down." Blue Bonnet still looked dazed as she turned to go into the house.

"Come in and see Kitty. The poor child is pretty blue."

"She was pretty red when I last saw her!" laughed Blue Bonnet. "I've something here to cheer her—a message from Sandy. She snubs him dreadfully, but he seems to enjoy it."

They found all the girls gathered about Kitty's bed, evidently in the midst of a serious discussion. Silence fell as Blue Bonnet entered.

"I can see out of one eye!" Kitty announced with forced gaiety.

"Praise be!" said Blue Bonnet. "Now you can see what Sandy sent for a farewell message." She held out the envelope.

"Open it please," said Kitty. "That boy is always up to mischief and I can't take any more risks. I cut one of his dances the other evening and he vowed vengeance."

Blue Bonnet obeyed while the other girls looked on with unconcealed interest. The envelope appeared to be empty, but when it was vigorously shaken upside down, something fell on to the counterpane. They all dove for it, but it was Debby who finally caught and held it up. It was a tiny square of note-paper, in the centre of which a knot of ribbon secured something bright and shining. It was a lock of Sandy's silky red hair. Under it was written: "A coal of fire. I forgive you."

Kitty laughed for the first time since her affliction had come upon her; and the girls blessed Sandy for his nonsense.

"May I borrow my granddaughter for a few minutes?" asked the Senora, looking in at the door. "Blue Bonnet, I've a letter here from your Aunt Lucinda."

An odd look came into Blue Bonnet's face,—Grandmother's voice held a hint of something important. She handed Sandy's memento to Kitty and forced a smile. "Put this in your memory-book, Kitty. When Sandy is president, you can point with pride to that coal of fire—they're likely, by then, to call it 'the fire of genius!'"

When she had left the room, Kitty looked out of her one good eye with a glance intended to be solemn. "Girls, I've a presentiment."

"What about,—Sandy?" asked Sarah.

"No, you silly,—except that he'll never be president! I'm thinking about Blue Bonnet,—I was just going to tell you when she came in. I don't believe she intends to go back with us."

Kitty's words produced even more of an effect than she had expected. For several minutes no one spoke, then Ruth said half irritably:

"If you can't have pleasanter presentiments than that, Kitty, I wish you wouldn't have them."

"I can't help it," Kitty declared. "She won't say a word about it. And every time we get on to the subject, she either begins to talk about something else, or leaves the room."

"I've noticed it, too," said Sarah, quietly.

The gloom on every countenance bore silent witness to the hold Blue Bonnet had on the affections of the We are Sevens.

"Woodford will be a stupid old hole without her," Kitty declared.

"Passing over your implied compliment to us," said Debby, "I agree with you."

Grandmother handed Blue Bonnet Aunt Lucinda's letter without comment; but watched the girl's face closely as she read. A characteristic letter it was, showing the fine mind and cultivation of the writer, yet like her, too, precise and rather formal in its wording. She was in Munich, enjoying the summer music festival. Nothing very important so far, Blue Bonnet concluded, and began to breathe more easily. But over the closing pages she sobered again.

"There is a rather remarkable pianist staying at this same pension," she wrote; "and she plays for us very often. Something in the charm and delicacy of her touch makes me think of Blue Bonnet's, when she plays her little 'Ave Maria.' I have talked with her about Blue Bonnet and she thinks with me that the child must have real talent for the piano. Fraeulein Schirmer is to teach music in a school for girls in Boston, this coming winter, and I think it would be an excellent plan to place Blue Bonnet right in the school. She is old enough now to appreciate the atmosphere of culture and refinement in such a place,—I am told that the first families of Boston send their daughters there—and she could have the advantage of attending the Symphony concerts.

"Woodford has nothing much to offer in the way of musical advantages, and I think Blue Bonnet should develop her talent in this line. She could come to us for the week-end always, and in that way we should not have to part with her altogether. But we can settle the matter when we are all in Woodford once more."

Blue Bonnet sighed as she finished and let the letter drop into her lap. "When they were all in Woodford once more." So Aunt Lucinda, too, took it for granted! She stirred a trifle resentfully.

"One would think I had signed a life-contract!" she thought.

Mrs. Clyde sought her granddaughter's eye anxiously. "Well, Blue Bonnet, what are you thinking?"

"I'm thinking—not for the first time either,—of something I once said to Alec. I wished, and keep on wishing—that there were two of me,—so that one might stay here on the ranch with Uncle Cliff, while the other was with you and Aunt Lucinda in Woodford, being educated."

Grandmother smiled and sighed in the same breath. "Suppose you leave me and Uncle Clifford and Aunt Lucinda out of the matter entirely. Just think how it would have appealed to—your mother."

The blue eyes turned swiftly from her grandmother's face to gaze out across the wide sweep of prairie. There was a long silence. When Blue Bonnet faced her grandmother again, her eyes were misty.

"I wish she were here to tell me. Somehow I can't make it seem right, either way. Will you wait and let me sleep on it, Grandmother? I'll tell you, as the Mexicans say—*manana*."

"To-morrow?"

"Well, *manana* with the Mexicans means almost any time in the future, but I'll make it—to-morrow."

Mrs. Clyde was silent, but the glance that followed Blue Bonnet as she left the room, was very wistful.

CHAPTER XXI

BLUE BONNET DECIDES

"I SAY, Blue Bonnet, wait for a fellow, won't you?"

Blue Bonnet waited, none too eagerly, while Alec caught up with her, and then, whistling to Don and Solomon, turned to resume her walk along the grassy bank of San Franciscito.

Alec surveyed her proud little profile for a few minutes in a sort of puzzled wonder, and finally as she kept on in the same unsociable manner, he began with determined friendliness:

"We've never yet taken the walk we planned, along the *rio*. Feel equal to it this morning?"

"There isn't time to go far. I told Grandmother I'd not be gone long," she returned carelessly.

"Another tea-party on?" This time he succeeded in bringing the old sparkle of laughter to her eyes.

"Not this time," she answered.

"Your parties have been a sort of continuous performance

this summer, haven't they?" he persisted, hoping to win her to a more conversational mood.

"And the summer is almost over,—did you ever know such a short vacation?"

"It's been the jolliest one I've ever had. And it is going to mean a lot to me all my life, Blue Bonnet."

They walked on in silence for a few minutes. Then Alec asked—"Do you remember the morning we first spoke of following this stream?"

"Yes,—and do you remember how we wondered what we would talk about on our next jaunt by the Woodford brook?"

He nodded. "I remember everything; that was the first day I told you I wasn't likely to be in Woodford next spring. It was only a day-dream then,—isn't it funny how things have come out?"

"Funny? Alec, you are the queerest boy. You've taken to talking in riddles lately, and I—I reckon I'm pretty slow at guessing riddles. We may as well have it out right now. I've been wanting to have a talk with you."

"Same here," returned Alec. "What's the matter, anyway? You've not been a bit like yourself the last few days."

"Don't you really know, Alec?" Blue Bonnet met his puzzled eyes very soberly.

"I honestly don't, Blue Bonnet."

"And haven't you felt the least little bit guilty about letting me write that letter to your grandfather?"

"Guilty?" Alec's tone expressed unaffected amazement. "Do you mean I ought to have written it myself? I'd have done it if you had hinted that you'd rather have me. Why didn't you say so?"

"You seemed so anxious to have me do it."

"And so I was. It seemed only right and proper that you should be the first to suggest the proposition. You're the owner of the Blue Bonnet ranch."

"What has that to do with it?"

"Well, I should think it had everything to do with it. I couldn't very well invite myself, could I?"

"Invite yourself? Oh, dear, now you're talking in riddles again."

"Well, Blue Bonnet, after you had invited me to spend two months on the ranch, it certainly took more courage than I possessed to suggest extending my visit for a year or two. You can see how much better it was for the suggestion to come from you. Grandfather has fallen right in with it and is making all arrangements with Mr. Ashe right now."

Blue Bonnet's eyes grew round with astonishment. "Do you mean to tell me that you are going to stay on the ranch a year or two?"

"If you and Mr. Ashe will stand for it. I want to stay till I outgrow being a weakling and grow into a real man. Till I'm as broad as a fellow my age should be and have a muscle bigger than a girl's. The two months here have already shown what two years is likely to do for me." Alec squared his shoulders and drew himself up as if already the example of brawn he longed to be.

"And do you mean to tell me that when you said you might not go back to Woodford, and that there was no college in store for Alec Trent you only meant—"

"Till I had the strength to go through with it, yes. I've had enough breakdowns. Why, what—"

"I wish you were a girl so that I could shake you!" Blue Bonnet's look was a queer mixture of relief and indignation. "Why couldn't you say so in the first place? When you kept making all those mysterious hints, I was wasting good, honest pity on you because I thought you were preparing for an early grave!"

Alec's peal of laughter showed how far from pitiable his state was. "Oh, Blue Bonnet, I wish I could tell that to Knight!"

"But didn't you hint?" she demanded.

"Of course I did. I was fishing for an invitation to make a good long visit to the Blue Bonnet ranch. Hardly likely, was it, that I was going to demand it boldly as a right?"

"Well, it would have saved me a heap of worry if you had. Why, Alec!" Blue Bonnet sank down on the bank to think it over. "What are you going to do on the ranch all winter?"

He threw himself on the grass beside her.

"I'm going to live, as far as possible, like Pinto Pete and Shady. I'm going to ride the range, go on the round-up this fall and next spring,—spend about fifteen hours a day in the open. And if I'm not as husky as a Texas cowboy by next summer, it won't be my fault. You know it's been my one wish, Blue

Bonnet, and this, I'm convinced is the way to get it."

"And college?"

"College can wait. I'd rather have biceps like Knight's than be a walking encyclopaedia!"

"Think of all the sympathy I've wasted!" Blue Bonnet laughed at herself.

"Oh, I don't know that it's all been wasted. I've deserved a good deal. I've been afraid Grandfather would be against the scheme—he's never been willing to admit that I wasn't as strong as I ought to be. I've only just begun myself to realize how good-for-nothing I used to feel most of the time. There's nothing like feeling able to shake your fist at all out-doors!"

Blue Bonnet smiled. "Then I needn't regret my letter?"

"Regret?—well, I should say not! You builded better than you knew. Getting Grandfather worried was just the right thing, though it sounds rather heartless to say it. Being worried, he came and saw and—I conquered!"

"Now I won't have to ask for an explanation of a very rude speech of yours."

"Was I rude—to you?" Alec looked up hastily.

"It sounded—rather queer, for you to rejoice over my not going back to Woodford," she answered.

"Meant purely as a compliment," he assured her. "It would be mighty jolly to have you here, Blue Bonnet."

She rose hurriedly. "Let's not go into that, please. Every time

I get pretty near a decision, some new argument bobs up on the other side. I'm dreadfully worried, Alec. But, thank goodness, you're off my mind!"

"I'll try to stay off, Blue Bonnet," he laughed as he followed her along the narrow path. "If you go back you'll write often, won't you? I shall depend on you—"

She made a movement of impatience. "I'm not going to cross bridges, Alec, till I come to them."

"I beg your pardon. I forgot that bridges are a touchy subject with you!"

They found Uncle Cliff and the General still absorbed in what appeared to be an interminable conversation. The General rose with old-fashioned courtesy as Blue Bonnet came up the veranda steps.

"What do you think of your new cowboy?" he asked, laying his hand affectionately on Alec's shoulder.

"We've just been exchanging opinions with each other," she said, with a sidelong glance at Alec.

"I'm going to miss the boy," General Trent continued. "The old house will be very dull and empty,—unless you make up your mind to be particularly neighborly, Miss Blue Bonnet."

Blue Bonnet colored and looked way. "I—I'll do my best if—"

"Will you walk down to the stable with me, Grandfather?" Alec asked quickly. "I've not shown you the little coyotes yet."

As the General walked away with his hand still on Alec's shoulder, Blue Bonnet turned to her uncle.

"Read this, will you please, Uncle? It came to-day."

He took Aunt Lucinda's letter, an odd expression growing around his mouth. But he opened it without speaking. Blue Bonnet sank into the hammock and watched him narrowly, —much as Grandmother had watched her as she read the same pages. She saw his lower teeth close on his mustache when he came to the significant part.

He lifted his eyes at last. "Well, Honey?"

"Well, Uncle?"

He sighed deeply. "Are you putting this up to me?"

She raised her shoulders in an expressive shrug. "I reckon you ought to have the deciding vote. I'm on the fence."

"Do you want to be a musician, Blue Bonnet?"

"I'd love to—if it weren't for all the practising!"

"Seems to me you play mighty well now."

"I'm very careless in my methods, Aunt Lucinda says."

Uncle Cliff winced. "None of the girls play as well as you do, Honey."

"I—I don't believe they do. But maybe, Uncle Cliff, that is a very good reason why I should go on with it. Maybe I really have talent."

"Wouldn't it be very lonesome off there in Boston? And won't it be mostly work and very little play?"

"I'm afraid it will. But, somehow, it's chiefly because it will be so much easier to stay on the ranch and be—desultory, as Aunt Lucinda says,—that I think I ought to go."

"I see, Honey. You *are* developing a New England conscience!"

"I wonder?" she pondered.

"I don't want you to do anything just because it's easier, Blue Bonnet," Uncle Cliff continued. "That wasn't your father's way."

"Nor your way, Uncle Cliff."

"I hope not, Blue Bonnet. That's why I'm going to stop arguing right here. It's my natural inclination to say 'stay with me, Honey, I need you.' But I know I don't,—I just want you. But what I want more is to have you do the thing that's best for Blue Bonnet Ashe,—the thing that will make you say in the end, 'I'm glad I did it!'" More moved than he cared to show, Clifford Ashe rose, and running down the veranda steps, strode off in the direction of the stable.

"Oh, dear!" thought Blue Bonnet, gazing after him. "In the language of the cowboys,—it's certainly up to me!"

When she went into her grandmother's room that night—the room that had been her mother's—Blue Bonnet found Benita acting as lady's maid, brushing Mrs. Clyde's long hair. The old nurse enjoyed nothing so much as waiting on the little Senora's mother,—unless it was babying the little Senora's daughter. As she stood in the doorway silently watching the

C. E. Jacobs & Edyth Ellerbeck Read

two, the sight of the rippling gray locks, fast whitening into snow, did more to sway Blue Bonnet than all the other array of arguments. Uncle Cliff wanted her; it was Grandmother who really needed her.

She tiptoed up back of Benita, but her grandmother had caught sight of her in the mirror and turned at her approach. Something in the expression of Blue Bonnet's eyes as she bent for the good-night kiss made Mrs. Clyde say hastily—

"What is it, dear?"

And Blue Bonnet, her tone reflecting the happiness her words gave, replied: "It isn't *manana* yet, but I can't wait to tell you—I'm going when you go, Grandmother."

When they looked up, Benita stood with her apron thrown over her face.

CHAPTER XXII

HASTA LA VISTA

THE We are Sevens were packing. An open trunk blocked each aisle between the six beds in the nursery; in Sarah's room two more were standing, half-filled, one reflecting the neatness and order of its owner, the other bearing silent witness to the fact that it belonged to Blue Bonnet Ashe.

"What are you doing with that old stick, Blue Bonnet?" asked Sarah, as she carefully folded her riding-skirt and laid tissue paper between the folds.

"Old stick, indeed! That's the alpenstock Knight cut for me and Sandy carved,—I've sawed off about six inches of it, though it broke my heart to do it. It's one of my dearest treasures and I'm going to take it to Woodford if I have to carry it all the way!" Blue Bonnet declared vigorously.

"I don't see anything so wonderful about it," Sarah returned. "There are plenty of old sticks just like it to be had around Woodford."

Blue Bonnet lifted indignant eyes. "As if any old Woodford stick could mean as much as this one. Why, this has the initials of every one in both camps carved on it, and every inch of it represents a good time. You've no sentiment, Sarah."

"I certainly haven't enough sentiment to make me rumple my best white dress with a clumsy old stick," Sarah replied.

"I reckon it ought to have gone in with my shoes, but it's too late now. How you do fuss over that riding-skirt, Sarah!"

"Well, if you want to know it, I've a lot of sentiment about that skirt. I wish I could take Comanche along, too."

Here Blue Bonnet amazed Sarah by jumping up and giving her a hug. "Oh, Sarah, I do love you for saying that! If you had been reconciled to riding that same old poke you had last year I'd have been so—disgusted. Won't the livery-man in Woodford open his eyes when Miss Blake demands a 'horse with some go in him'—! The inhabitants of the town will get a few thrills too, I reckon."

"Do you think it will be proper for us to ride there the way we ride here?" Sarah asked eagerly.

"Astride? We'll make it proper! It's the only humane way, Uncle says—a side-saddle is a downright cruelty. And I don't see why a parson's daughter shouldn't set the fashion."

"Then Ruth will get a chance to wear her riding-skirt after all—her heart will be stronger after a while. I've hated to ride when she couldn't, but she has insisted upon our going."

"That's just like you, you unselfish old dear! But Ruth told me that it was the next best thing to riding herself, to see you on Comanche."

"Did she?" asked Sarah; and then hid her face in the trunk so that Blue Bonnet should not see how pleased she was.

They were to leave in the morning, and trunks were to be sent to the station this very afternoon. Already Uncle Joe was hovering about, rope in hand, waiting to give the final touch to the baggage. He had found it necessary to keep very busy these last few days.

"We might have seen this coming," he said disconsolately to Mr. Ashe, as the latter sat smoking a solitary pipe on the front veranda. "Let young folks get runnin' with young folks, and they're never again contented alone."

"It isn't *young* folks that's taking Blue Bonnet this time, Joe." Mr. Ashe glanced in to where a silver head showed just inside the window. "*Her* girl never went back to her from Texas, and I reckon it's only right she should have her share of Elizabeth's daughter."

Uncle Joe looked sober. "You're right, Cliff." Then, as if determined to look on the bright side of things, "We'll have the boy for company."

"Yes, and there'll be more letters. She'll tell him things she wouldn't be likely to write to two old fellows." And with this crumb of comfort the "two old fellows" were forced to content themselves.

Blue Bonnet was up at daybreak next morning, and, sitting on the top rail of the pasture fence, watched the sun rise out of the prairie. Don and Solomon eyed her expectantly.

"Our last sunrise on the ranch, Solomon, for ever and ever so long,—we're off to Massachusetts this very morning. And it's a Pullman for me and a baggage-car for you—no private car this time! But I'll come and see you at every station and see that you have exercise. Poor dog, I wonder how you'll like the 'resumption of discipline'—as Alec calls it? We're going back to Aunt Lucinda, you know, Solomon, and Aunt Lucinda's strong for discipline."

Her eyes wandered off toward the distant hills and then away across the wind-swept, rolling prairie. How would it seem to be back again among houses, tall houses with trim door-yards and clipped hedges,—houses so close one couldn't throw a stone without "breaking a window or a tradition"—?

Some one was whistling "All the Blue Bonnets are over the Border." She looked up as Alec came towards her.

"Do I intrude upon a solemn hour?" he asked.

"The solemn hour has ticked its last second. I've said good-bye to everything and everybody,—except Texas and Massachusetts. Come with me to see those infants."

Hardly infants any longer, however. Long-tailed, with erect silky ears and coats that stood out shaggily from their fattening sides, the coyotes were fast growing into big, clumsy dogs.

"You'll look after them, won't you, Alec?" Blue Bonnet asked anxiously.

"That I will," he promised.

"And you'll write me often about—everything? And see that Uncle Cliff doesn't smoke too much, and that Uncle Joe takes his rheumatism medicine—"

"Trust me!" Alec knew better than to smile at such a moment. "And in turn, Blue Bonnet, you'll give an eye to

Grandfather, won't you?"

They shook hands on it solemnly, and went in to breakfast.

Kitty, her face restored to its usual milky-whiteness, and looking very pretty in her jaunty travelling-suit, met them at the door. Peering over her shoulder stood Ruth—a sunburned Ruth with bright eyes and a rounder curve to her cheek than it had worn two weeks before.

"We were afraid you had decided to run off and hide at the last minute," said Kitty, slipping her arm around Blue Bonnet as if determined not to risk losing her a second time.

"I was only—saying good-bye," said Blue Bonnet soberly.

"Blue Bonnet is like more than one famous prima donna," said Alec, "she has made half a dozen 'positively last' fare-well tours!"

They were off at last. Distributed equally between the buckboard and one of the farm-wagons, the We are Sevens, Grandmother Clyde, General Trent and Uncle Joe went ahead. Blue Bonnet, Alec, and Uncle Cliff followed on horseback.

As they neared the bridge Blue Bonnet drew rein, and, turning in the saddle, glanced back for a last look at the weather-stained old ranch-house. The cowboys and most of the Mexicans, who had gathered to say good-bye to the Senorita and her "amigos" from Massachusetts, were already scattering about the work of the day. But in the doorway the faithful Benita still stood, waving her apron.

Blue Bonnet's eyes filled.

"Good-bye, old house, good-bye, Benita," she said, and then added softly: "*Hasta la vista!*"

THE END

Choose from Thousands of 1stWorldLibrary Classics By

A. M. Barnard	Booth Tarkington	Edward Everett Hale
Ada Leverson	Boyd Cable	Edward J. O'Biren
Adolphus William Ward	Bram Stoker	Edward S. Ellis
Aesop	C. Collodi	Edwin L. Arnold
Agatha Christie	C. E. Orr	Eleanor Atkins
Alexander Aaronsohn	C. M. Ingleby	Eleanor Hallowell Abbott
Alexander Kielland	Carolyn Wells	Eliot Gregory
Alexandre Dumas	Catherine Parr Traill	Elizabeth Gaskell
Alfred Gatty	Charles A. Eastman	Elizabeth McCracken
Alfred Ollivant	Charles Amory Beach	Elizabeth Von Arnim
Alice Duer Miller	Charles Dickens	Ellem Key
Alice Turner Curtis	Charles Dudley Warner	Emerson Hough
Alice Dunbar	Charles Farrar Browne	Emilie F. Carlen
Allen Chapman	Charles Ives	Emily Bronte
Alleyne Ireland	Charles Kingsley	Emily Dickinson
Ambrose Bierce	Charles Klein	Enid Bagnold
Amelia E. Barr	Charles Hanson Towne	Enilor Macartney Lane
Amory H. Bradford	Charles Lathrop Pack	Erasmus W. Jones
Andrew Lang	Charles Romyn Dake	Ernie Howard Pie
Andrew McFarland Davis	Charles Whibley	Ethel May Dell
Andy Adams	Charles Willing Beale	Ethel Turner
Angela Brazil	Charlotte M. Braeme	Ethel Watts Mumford
Anna Alice Chapin	Charlotte M. Yonge	Eugene Sue
Anna Sewell	Charlotte Perkins Stetson	Eugenie Foa
Annie Besant	Clair W. Hayes	Eugene Wood
Annie Hamilton Donnell	Clarence Day Jr.	Eustace Hale Ball
Annie Payson Call	Clarence E. Mulford	Evelyn Everett-green
Annie Roe Carr	Clemence Housman	Everard Cotes
Annonaymous	Confucius	F. H. Cheley
Anton Chekhov	Coningsby Dawson	F. J. Cross
Archibald Lee Fletcher	Cornelis DeWitt Wilcox	F. Marion Crawford
Arnold Bennett	Cyril Burleigh	Fannie E. Newberry
Arthur C. Benson	D. H. Lawrence	Federick Austin Ogg
Arthur Conan Doyle	Daniel Defoe	Ferdinand Ossendowski
Arthur M. Winfield	David Garnett	Fergus Hume
Arthur Ransome	Dinah Craik	Florence A. Kilpatrick
Arthur Schnitzler	Don Carlos Janes	Fremont B. Deering
Arthur Train	Donald Keyhoe	Francis Bacon
Atticus	Dorothy Kilner	Francis Darwin
B.H. Baden-Powell	Dougan Clark	Frances Hodgson Burnett
B. M. Bower	Douglas Fairbanks	Frances Parkinson Keyes
B. C. Chatterjee	E. Nesbit	Frank Gee Patchin
Baroness Emmuska Orczy	E. P. Roe	Frank Harris
Baroness Orczy	E. Phillips Oppenheim	Frank Jewett Mather
Basil King	E. S. Brooks	Frank L. Packard
Bayard Taylor	Earl Barnes	Frank V. Webster
Ben Macomber	Edgar Rice Burroughs	Frederic Stewart Isham
Bertha Muzzy Bower	Edith Van Dyne	Frederick Trevor Hill
Bjornstjerne Bjornson	Edith Wharton	Frederick Winslow Taylor

Friedrich Kerst
Friedrich Nietzsche
Fyodor Dostoyevsky
G.A. Henty
G.K. Chesterton
Gabrielle E. Jackson
Garrett P. Serviss
Gaston Leroux
George A. Warren
George Ade
Geroge Bernard Shaw
George Cary Eggleston
George Durston
George Ebers
George Eliot
George Gissing
George MacDonald
George Meredith
George Orwell
George Sylvester Viereck
George Tucker
George W. Cable
George Wharton James
Gertrude Atherton
Gordon Casserly
Grace E. King
Grace Gallatin
Grace Greenwood
Grant Allen
Guillermo A. Sherwell
Gulielma Zollinger
Gustav Flaubert
H. A. Cody
H. B. Irving
H.C. Bailey
H. G. Wells
H. H. Munro
H. Irving Hancock
H. R. Naylor
H. Rider Haggard
H. W. C. Davis
Haldeman Julius
Hall Caine
Hamilton Wright Mabie
Hans Christian Andersen
Harold Avery
Harold McGrath
Harriet Beecher Stowe
Harry Castlemon
Harry Coghill
Harry Houidini

Hayden Carruth
Helent Hunt Jackson
Helen Nicolay
Hendrik Conscience
Hendy David Thoreau
Henri Barbusse
Henrik Ibsen
Henry Adams
Henry Ford
Henry Frost
Henry James
Henry Jones Ford
Henry Seton Merriman
Henry W Longfellow
Herbert A. Giles
Herbert Carter
Herbert N. Casson
Herman Hesse
Hildegard G. Frey
Homer
Honore De Balzac
Horace B. Day
Horace Walpole
Horatio Alger Jr.
Howard Pyle
Howard R. Garis
Hugh Lofting
Hugh Walpole
Humphry Ward
Ian Maclaren
Inez Haynes Gillmore
Irving Bacheller
Isabel Cecilia Williams
Isabel Hornibrook
Israel Abrahams
Ivan Turgenev
J.G.Austin
J. Henri Fabre
J. M. Barrie
J. M. Walsh
J. Macdonald Oxley
J. R. Miller
J. S. Fletcher
J. S. Knowles
J. Storer Clouston
J. W. Duffield
Jack London
Jacob Abbott
James Allen
James Andrews
James Baldwin

James Branch Cabell
James DeMille
James Joyce
James Lane Allen
James Lane Allen
James Oliver Curwood
James Oppenheim
James Otis
James R. Driscoll
Jane Abbott
Jane Austen
Jane L. Stewart
Janet Aldridge
Jens Peter Jacobsen
Jerome K. Jerome
Jessie Graham Flower
John Buchan
John Burroughs
John Cournos
John F. Kennedy
John Gay
John Glasworthy
John Habberton
John Joy Bell
John Kendrick Bangs
John Milton
John Philip Sousa
John Taintor Foote
Jonas Lauritz Idemil Lie
Jonathan Swift
Joseph A. Altsheler
Joseph Carey
Joseph Conrad
Joseph E. Badger Jr
Joseph Hergesheimer
Joseph Jacobs
Jules Vernes
Julian Hawthrone
Julie A Lippmann
Justin Huntly McCarthy
Kakuzo Okakura
Karle Wilson Baker
Kate Chopin
Kenneth Grahame
Kenneth McGaffey
Kate Langley Bosher
Kate Langley Bosher
Katherine Cecil Thurston
Katherine Stokes
L. A. Abbot
L. T. Meade

L. Frank Baum
Latta Griswold
Laura Dent Crane
Laura Lee Hope
Laurence Housman
Lawrence Beasley
Leo Tolstoy
Leonid Andreyev
Lewis Carroll
Lewis Sperry Chafer
Lilian Bell
Lloyd Osbourne
Louis Hughes
Louis Joseph Vance
Louis Tracy
Louisa May Alcott
Lucy Fitch Perkins
Lucy Maud Montgomery
Luther Benson
Lydia Miller Middleton
Lyndon Orr
M. Corvus
M. H. Adams
Margaret E. Sangster
Margret Howth
Margaret Vandercook
Margaret W. Hungerford
Margret Penrose
Maria Edgeworth
Maria Thompson Daviess
Mariano Azuela
Marion Polk Angellotti
Mark Overton
Mark Twain
Mary Austin
Mary Catherine Crowley
Mary Cole
Mary Hastings Bradley
Mary Roberts Rinehart
Mary Rowlandson
M. Wollstonecraft Shelley
Maud Lindsay
Max Beerbohm
Myra Kelly
Nathaniel Hawthrone
Nicolo Machiavelli
O. F. Walton
Oscar Wilde

Owen Johnson
P.G. Wodehouse
Paul and Mabel Thorne
Paul G. Tomlinson
Paul Severing
Percy Brebner
Percy Keese Fitzhugh
Peter B. Kyne
Plato
Quincy Allen
R. Derby Holmes
R. L. Stevenson
R. S. Ball
Rabindranath Tagore
Rahul Alvares
Ralph Bonehill
Ralph Henry Barbour
Ralph Victor
Ralph Waldo Emmerson
Rene Descartes
Ray Cummings
Rex Beach
Rex E. Beach
Richard Harding Davis
Richard Jefferies
Richard Le Gallienne
Robert Barr
Robert Frost
Robert Gordon Anderson
Robert L. Drake
Robert Lansing
Robert Lynd
Robert Michael Ballantyne
Robert W. Chambers
Rosa Nouchette Carey
Rudyard Kipling
Saint Augustine
Samuel B. Allison
Samuel Hopkins Adams
Sarah Bernhardt
Sarah C. Hallowell
Selma Lagerlof
Sherwood Anderson
Sigmund Freud
Standish O'Grady
Stanley Weyman
Stella Benson
Stella M. Francis

Stephen Crane
Stewart Edward White
Stijn Streuvels
Swami Abhedananda
Swami Parmananda
T. S. Ackland
T. S. Arthur
The Princess Der Ling
Thomas A. Janvier
Thomas A Kempis
Thomas Anderton
Thomas Bailey Aldrich
Thomas Bulfinch
Thomas De Quincey
Thomas Dixon
Thomas H. Huxley
Thomas Hardy
Thomas More
Thornton W. Burgess
U. S. Grant
Upton Sinclair
Valentine Williams
Various Authors
Vaughan Kester
Victor Appleton
Victor G. Durham
Victoria Cross
Virginia Woolf
Wadsworth Camp
Walter Camp
Walter Scott
Washington Irving
Wilbur Lawton
Wilkie Collins
Willa Cather
Willard F. Baker
William Dean Howells
William le Queux
W. Makepeace Thackeray
William W. Walter
William Shakespeare
Winston Churchill
Yei Theodora Ozaki
Yogi Ramacharaka
Young E. Allison
Zane Grey